Lamp

Dr. Jaerock Lee's
one-minute columns

Lamp

Dr. Jaerock Lee's
one-minute columns

"Your word is a lamp to my feet and a light to my path."
(Psalm 119:105)

Lamp by Dr. Jaerock Lee
Published by Urim Books (Representative: Seongkeon Vin)
235-3, Guro-dong 3, Guro-gu, Seoul, Korea
www.urimbooks.com

Unless otherwise noted, all Scripture quotations are taken from the Holy Bible, NEW AMERICAN STANDARD BIBLE, ®, Copyright © 1960, 1962, 1963, 1968, 1971, 1972, 1973, 1975, 1977, 1995 by The Lockman Foundation. Used by permission.

Copyright © 2012 by Dr. Jaerock Lee
ISBN: 978-89-7557-638-6
Translation Copyright © 2012 by Dr. Esther K. Chung. Used by permission.

Previously published into Korean in 2011 by Urim Books in Seoul, Korea

First Published July 2012

Edited by Dr. Geumsun Vin
Designed by Editorial Bureau of Urim Books
Printed by Yewon Printing Company
For more information contact: urimbook@hotmail.com

Prologue

I give thanks and glory to God who had led me to publish this book. It was already more than ten years that my columns have been published in Korean major daily newspapers such as *The Chosun Ilbo, The Hankuk Ilbo, The Joongang Ilbo,* and *The Donga Ilbo.* It has been my pleasure to share the wisdom gained and the emotions experienced during my life as well as my ministry through the forementioned newspapers.

I was very pleased by the news that my columns have comforted the hearts of people of all ages from students to young adults and to the elderly and that they have provided them with 'bread for their souls.' Thinking about their faces and with the desire to share grace with more people, I have published this book.

This book is divided in seven parts that describe the love

of God who created the heavens and the earth and all things in them with expectation of gaining His true children whose hearts resemble His own. This book contains things necessary for our lives including the love of God, the mystery of the Creation, solutions to life's problems, the life that gives out the fragrance and light of Christ, and the ways to receive heavenly wisdom.

I hope this small book will serve as a lighthouse to help people navigate as they sail on their life's journey and a ray of light to travelers who walk at night. I believe that this book will encourage those who have lost their strength and just sit still, to stand up again and move ahead. I believe that it will play a role as a guidance tool that will lead to answers and blessings for the many souls who are wandering aimlessly.

I extend my sincere thanks to those who have devoted

themselves to collecting material, planning, editing, designing, and printing this book. I pray in the name of the Lord that the lamp of peace, happiness, joy, and true life will more brightly light the hearts of readers.

April 2011

Jaerock Lee

Table of
Contents

Prologue

Part 2

Clear Sky, Blue Sea

Part 3

The Gifts Given to Us

Part 6

Happiness and Sharing Love

Part 7

Hope for Heaven

"Then God said, 'Let there be light'; and there was light.
God saw that the light was good; and God separated the light from the darkness."

Genesis 1:3-4

Part 1

With the Light

Spiritual Thoughts

"For the mind set on the flesh is death,
  but the mind set on the Spirit is life and peace."
(Romans 8:6)

Happiness depends on how we think. In a certain situation, we can be happy or unhappy depending on our way of thinking. Seeing a half glass of water some people may think, "The glass is half empty." Seeing the same glass others may think, "The glass is half full." This is like two sides of the same coin. It is up to us to choose one side. The more we accept negative thoughts the worse the situation may become. On the other hand, when we look on the bright side and live a faithful life in God, we can overcome any difficulty.

The Origin of the Light

"This is the message we have heard from Him and announce to you, that God is Light, and in Him there is no darkness at all."
(1 John 1:5)

There are two kinds of people. One pursues the light like plants which grow toward light and the other pursues darkness. The attributes of the light are goodness, love, and truth. The attributes of the darkness are sin, unrighteousness, and untruth.

No matter how dark it may be, the darkness can only vanish where the light shines and where light shines truth is naturally revealed. It is much the same for evil men who seem to prosper for the moment. In the end truth will be revealed and goodness will achieve the final victory. That is because God the Creator, the Origin of the light, controls the realm of the light.

God's Design

"For by Him all things were created, both in the heavens and on earth,
  visible and invisible, whether thrones or dominions or rulers or authorities—
  all things have been created through Him and for Him."
(Colossians 1:16)

A design is necessary to create even the
smallest building. There was a perfect design
to create the earth as well. The design was
held in the heart of God. With His amazing
wisdom and power of creation, God created
the earth as He had designed. Humans can feel
His delicate touch by observing all the things
in the solar system. From the rotation and
revolution of the earth, the ebb and flow of the
tides, and the movement of winds and clouds,
we can observe His wisdom and power. It is
not fruit of coincidence. God the Creator
placed all things in their proper places and set
them to move in order and harmony.

The Solar System and the Earth

"Then God said, 'Let there be lights in the expanse
of the heavens to separate the day from the night,
and let them be for signs and for seasons and for days and years.'"
(Genesis 1:14)

Mercury, Venus, Earth, Mars, Jupiter, Saturn, Uranus, and Neptune are able to exist in the place where they are because they have maintained the proper size and the appropriate distance from each other. In other words, they were created so that they can balance pull and push between each other, even if it is not visible. If the sun or other planets were bigger or smaller than they are now, the whole solar system would be affected. Among them, the Earth is situated in the optimal location for living creatures to exist. Nothing can live on Mercury, which is closest to the sun or on Venus which is just a little farther or on Mars, which is a little further from the sun than the Earth. The Earth is just where it needs to be. Observing this, we see that the Solar System was not formed by coincidence, but created with God's amazing wisdom and power.

A Voyage of Life

"Then they were glad because they were quiet,
so He guided them to their desired haven."
(Psalm 107:30)

Throughout the Pacific Ocean there are many places where rocky coastal areas exist. To sail safely there, you have to sail at an angle where the light of three lighthouses overlap and look like one lighthouse. Likewise, only when we set a goal angled to line up with God the Creator can we lead a peaceful life. When our goal does not agree with God's, we will wander meeting with many problems like rocks in the sea. However, when we set our course on God who created the heavens and the earth and all humanity and set our goals angled toward Him, He will drive away the gusty winds and cause the waves to become calm. He will help our sailing through life to be safe.

Creation and Science

"By faith we understand that the worlds
were prepared by the word of God,
so that what is seen was not made out of things which are visible."
(Hebrews 11:3)

We benefit from high-technology and lead lives of convenience because science and technology have been developed so remarkably. However, no matter how striking the development is, no one can create something out of nothing. Humans need something to create something new. Thus, not science, industry nor even human civilization can be considered 'fruit of creation', but only something that is improvement or invention stemming from something that has already existed. The work of creation, which creates something out of nothing, is in the dominion only of God and what only God the Creator can do.

The Frequency of the Heart

"Have this attitude in yourselves which
  was also in Christ Jesus."
(Philippians 2:5)

To listen to a specific radio program we have
to tune in that particular station's frequency.
If we tune in another radio frequency we
cannot hear the right sound because of
noise or another radio broadcasting coming
from the radio. Likewise, when we 'tune'
our heart's 'frequency' to the Word of God
we can receive only thoughts of goodness
and truth. We accept untruthful thought
and practice evil deeds, however, when we
'tune' our heart to evil things. Therefore, we
must tune our hearts to God's heart that is
goodness itself all the time.

Prayer of Love

"Let us not lose heart in doing good,
  for in due time we will reap if we do not grow weary."
(Galatians 6:9)

When I was an atheist I suffered from many diseases for seven years. There was nothing but death waiting for me. One day, my second eldest sister visited my home from the far-distant place where she lived and said, "I have a place I really want to go. Please guide me there." I felt her eagerness to go there because she asked me to lead the way for her even though I was very sick. So I took her there though I had to rely on a cane to walk. When I arrived there a number of people were praying. I happened to bend my knees without really knowing what I was doing. At that very moment God healed me of all my diseases at once. Afterwards, I heard an unexpected fact that my second eldest sister had prayed for me for a long time. With the strength of her prayer, I could come before God and accept Jesus Christ. As the Psalm 125:6 says, *"Those who sow in tears shall reap with joyful shouting,"* the prayer of love for souls will surely yield its fruit.

The Shortcut to Happiness

"And to keep the LORD's commandments and His statutes
which I am commanding you today for your good?"
(Deuteronomy 10:13)

In the past I used to enjoy reading martial
arts novels. Characters in the novels sought
revenge on those who wronged them. I
thought they did so out of righteousness.
But I realized after believing in God my
righteousness and His righteousness are
totally different. I used to think that paying
evil back with evil was fair enough, but God
tells us to love our enemies. Realizing the love
of the cross I started to follow only God's
righteousness. As time went by I enjoyed
peace in my heart and blessings increased.
True righteousness is to live according to the
Word written in the Bible. It is the shortcut
to happiness.

Speck and Log

"Why do you look at the speck that is in your brother's eye,
but do not notice the log that is in your own eye?"
(Luke 6:41)

Cars have mirrors to help drivers see around
them and drive safely. But still there are
dead spots that don't come into view.
Likewise, we might have a shortcoming
that is not easy to spot in ourselves. Rather
than discovering their own shortcomings
and correcting them, there are some people
who see only the faults of others. When
they find the speck of a small fault of others
they immediately point it out while they
cannot see the serious evil in themselves. It
is a wise man who checks if he has a greater
shortcoming and changes himself when he
sees the shortcomings of others.

Let's Not Think It's a Joke

"Incline your ear and hear the words of the wise,
  and apply your mind to my knowledge."
(Proverbs 22:17)

The teachings of elderly people who have a lot of knowledge and experience are of much benefit to our lives. So then, is not the Word of God the Almighty much more beneficial? The Bible talks about people who disrespected God's Word. For example, when Lot's sons-in-law heard that Sodom and Gomorrah were extremely corrupt in morals and would be punished and destroyed by God, they thought it was just a joke. Lot's wife didn't listen attentively to the word telling them 'not to look back.' As a result, Lot's sons-in-law were destroyed in the city and his wife became a pillar of salt. No matter how much God wants to give us good things, if we consider His Word as though it were a joke we cannot receive them. On the other hand, those who open their hearts and believe Him, they will be guided to the way of salvation and blessings.

Not Accusation, But Forgiveness

"For if you forgive others for their transgressions,
 your heavenly Father will also forgive you."
(Matthew 6:14)

Nowadays, egoism is rampant. Many people
file suits for a mere trifle. Sometimes it is even
their wife, parents, or children whom they
file law suits against. Jesus told us, *"Whoever
slaps on your right cheek, turn the other
to him also"* (Matthew 5:39). He urged us
to practice only goodness without repaying
evil with evil. If you think it's unreasonable
to forgive and understand others, just think
about the love of God who sent His one and
only Son to the earth for the salvation of all
human beings. When you believe from the
bottom of the heart that such a great love has
been given to you, how can you not forgive
and love others?

The Two Are the Same

"There is only one Lawgiver and Judge,
the One who is able to save and to destroy;
but who are you who judge your neighbor?"
(James 4:12)

Just as the boughs bearing more fruit are bent lower, those who have greater faith have more humble hearts. Such people don't carelessly pass judgment on others either. However, among diligent Christians there are some who pass judgment on others without knowing it. For instance, when such a person sees someone not serving his neighbor with love, he might think, 'Oh, he still has hatred in his heart.' But, the one who has hatred and the other who passes judgment both live outside the Word. Only God is the Judge. So we must not judge others.

Better than A Hundred Words

"For we are a fragrance of Christ to God among those
who are being saved and among those who are perishing."
(2 Corinthians 2:15)

People of faith have their own fragrance.
For example, they give out the fragrance of
the heart that shows mercy to those who
fail in the world, the sick, the neglected,
and those who haven't met God. Most
people welcome or want to move close to
successful men while they turn their backs on
those who fail. But, men of faith pray with
warm hearts and encourage those who lose
heart and have diseases. The fragrance of a
merciful heart wipes away the tears of weary
men and testifies to the love of God with
stronger fragrance than a hundred words of
consolation.

First Priority and Second Priority

"So do not be like them;
  for your Father knows what you need before you ask Him."
(Matthew 6:8)

A few years ago, around 300 dolphins encountered disaster when they died while following sardines into a small bay. We sometimes lose a big thing pursuing a trivial matter. We have to know which the first priority is and which the second priority is not to make such mistakes. God promises He will add all things to us when we first seek His kingdom and His righteousness. When we prioritize wealth and fame we might fail. But when we work diligently for souls' salvation and live in the Word of God, wealth and fame naturally follow.

The Trait of Falsehood

People often add other words to the truth
or subtract some truth from it. Let's say your
friend eats too much of what you like and
you have only little left. You might say to
him, "Hey, you ate all of it" or "You left me
nothing to eat." Most people don't think it's a
lie, but it is definitely an attribute of untruth.
If we don't cast away such an attribute
completely we might tell a lie that causes
harm to others in an emergency situation.
Only when we fill our hearts with honesty
and truth in the small parts can we reach the
perfect level of truth.

Unshakable Peace

"Those who love Your law have great peace,
and nothing causes them to stumble."
(Psalm 119:165)

Meditation is like the process where dirty water becomes clean water because particles of dirt sink to the bottom of a cup. Your anger and hatred are eased and you regain peace when you close your eyes and concentrate. Just as the dirt rises up again when we shake the cup, impurities of the heart reappear under certain conditions. Fundamentally, to have true peace we have to get rid of evil from the heart. When we have a good and clean heart without evil we can have peace under any circumstances. It's just like there is no dirt in pure clean water.

Renewed Personality

"And have put on the new self who is being renewed
to a true knowledge according to the image
of the One who created him."
(Colossians 3:10)

We sometimes hesitate to do something because of our personality. John, who stayed near Jesus and reclined on Jesus' bosom in the picture called 'The Last Supper', was given the name 'Boanerges' which means "Son of Thunder." However, by the love of the crucifixion and the grace of redemption he changed into a person who was called the 'Apostle of love'. In this same way, those who realized God's love from the bottom of the heart can resemble Jesus Christ. Knowing this, we can change our personalities in order to live more valuable lives.

Which Way is Better?

"The heart of the wise instructs his mouth
and adds persuasiveness to his lips."
(Proverbs 16:23)

Compliments have a great effect on our lives. There are two kinds of parents in the church. When their children chat during the service, one kind of parents scold them saying, "God isn't pleased with the way you are behaving." The other kind of parents say, "You know that when you offer the service with a good attitude God will be pleased and give you rewards." In the former case, children might become disheartened thinking 'God is sad because of me and now He doesn't love me anymore.' In the latter case, children actively try to live in the Word of God thinking 'God is pleased and wants to give me good things.' Then, which of these ways is the better to apply to our lives?

The Words of Consideration

"Let your speech always be with grace,
  as though seasoned with salt..."
(Colossians 4:6)

Some vessels are made up of hard materials.
The more they are vigorously polished the
shinier they become. But there are vessels
formed from weaker materials. Such vessels
will break if a little too much power is
applied to them. In the same manner, people
have different vessels. Some have a strong
heart, but the others don't. So we have to be
careful when we give advice to others even if
we do it out of love. Also, even if you act or
speak for others, it might rather hurt their
feelings. We have to understand their hearts,
situations and conditions and take them into
consideration first before acting or speaking.

Although We Know
the Right Thing to Do

"Therefore, to one who knows and does not do it, to him it is sin."
(James 4:17)

There were some professional baseball players who purposely threw a game in exchange for money from gamblers. They were caught and received punishment. At that time, other players who didn't join in, but earnestly played in the game, also received the same punishment. This is because they knew the right thing to do and they may even have been able to stop the incident from happening, but they did nothing. In the same way, some people just silently observe others' wrongdoings and though they know how to keep it from happening they choose to do nothing because they know the possible personal disadvantages and repercussions. But it is said in James 4:17, *"Therefore, to one who knows the right thing to do and does not do it, to him it is sin."* We have to actively do goodness all the time resembling God who is goodness itself.

Removing the Causes

"Therefore if anyone is in Christ, he is a new creature;
the old things passed away; behold, new things have come."
(2 Corinthians 5:17)

Atopic dermatitis occurs because internal
factors in one's body confuse the immune
system and results in an extreme reaction of
the body to a regular stimulus. Therefore, it
is important to get rid of fundamental cause
to heal this disease. It is the same with anger
or agitation. People just blame something
on others saying "That person really irritates
me..." or "I can't do anything else but get
angry." But all the causes are brought in
themselves. In other words, your anger comes
out not because there is an external stimulus
but because you have anger in you. We can
have peace like a calm lake when we get
rid of fundamental root of anger and have
gentleness in our hearts.

Situation Depends on Hearts

"...let us also lay aside every encumbrance
and the sin which so easily entangles us,
and let us run with endurance the race that is set before us."
(Hebrews 12:1)

People run in the gym. There are two racers:
one who runs carrying a large rock in his arms
and the other who runs carrying nothing.
Who do you think can run faster? Of course,
the latter can run faster. The person who runs
with the rock cannot help but struggle while
running. In much the same way, we have hard
time when we have hearts hardened like stone.
With such hearts we can't embrace others
and we bear ill-feeling and easily quarrel over
something that is trivial. But, when we have
the heart of Jesus Christ that is gentle like
cotton, we can embrace others with love and
there is no quarrelling. We can peacefully run
unencumbered in the race of life.

Wise and Strong Men

"But the humble will inherit the land and
will delight themselves in abundant prosperity."
(Psalm 37:11)

It can never be said that the Omnipotent God is weak. But some people say God and Jesus seem to be weak because God tells us to 'offer our left cheek when someone slaps us on our right cheek' and Jesus never 'quarreled or cried out.' But it was because of this love and gentleness of Jesus that He was able to completely fulfill God's will through His crucifixion and resurrection. We need to be able to recognize true strength because we need to follow the one who is able to break down the hardness of the heart and allow for us to gain gentleness. In humble gentleness we can become truly wise and strong individuals who are able to change weaknesses into strengths.

"God made the expanse, and separated the waters which were below
the expanse from the waters which were above the expanse;
and it was so. God called the expanse heaven.
And there was evening and there was morning, a second day."

Genesis 1:7-8

Part 2

Clear Sky, Blue Sea

The Reason the Sky Is Blue

"By the word of the LORD the heavens were made,
  and by the breath of His mouth all their host."
(Psalm 33:6)

When looking at the clear blue sky with no
spot to be seen, we feel like our hearts are
being brightened and purified. On the other
hand, we feel depressed or have negative
thoughts when we look at the sky that is
overcast with low lying grey clouds. Our
hearts are influenced by the color of the sky.
That's why God didn't make the sky yellow,
red, or purple. He made it blue. The color
'blue' makes people feel composed and gives
feelings of peace and hope. God offers his
love so that we look up into the clear blue sky
and think, 'I will lead a clear and pure life like
the sky.'

Extraordinary Rainbows

"And He who was sitting was like a jasper stone
 and a sardius in appearance;
 and there was a rainbow around the throne,
 like an emerald in appearance."
(Revelation 4:3)

After punishing the world with water in the time
of Noah, God showed a rainbow as the sign of His
promise that He would not judge the world with
water again. Through the rainbow He showed
His love. In general, rainbows appear on the side
opposite to the sun after it rains. But it's hard to
see rainbows nowadays because smog caused by air
pollution often makes it hard for us to distinguish
rainbows with the naked eye. But, if God works we
can always see rainbows. In the morning, at night,
even on a day with no clouds we can see them.
There are even various and extraordinary shapes of
rainbows: circular, linear, and symmetric rainbows.
They appear as the sign of God's being with us. God
often proves Himself through wonders, signs, and
power that can't be explained through science.

The Mystery of Water

"For from Him and through Him and to Him are all things.
To Him be the glory forever."
(Romans 11:36)

When we think about things on the earth, we can't help but notice that everything had to have been elaborately designed by someone. Water in particular is different from other substances in terms of its densities. As a solid, water is less dense than as a liquid. Because of the density difference, ice floats on water. It is ice floating on water that enables many forms of marine life in the Polar Regions to survive. Ice can be said to shut off external thermal effects so that the temperature of the water beneath remains above freezing. Also the water in the vessel named 'the Earth' ought to be stagnant. But with just the right amount of salt in the water and the ebb and flow of tides, it keeps it from stagnating and allows all creatures to live. Thinking of such things, we can realize that the world has not been created by a series of coincidences, but by the power of the Creator, and it is He who set it in perfect balance and harmony.

The Ark of Noah

"If indeed you continue in the faith firmly established and steadfast,
and not moved away from the hope of the gospel that you have heard, ..."
(Colossians 1:23)

It is said that the ark that Noah and his family boarded during the judgment of flood thousands of years ago was found on Ararat Mountains in Turkey. One of the reasons the ark endured the great flood was that the ark was made of a very strong wood, gopher wood. While sailing on the sea of life we need strength like the gopher wood. However, it doesn't mean our personality should be strong. It means we have to have a firm and righteous heart with no change. Just as the ark of Noah endured the flood and protected those in it until they faced a new world, we can reach the gate of Heaven by achieving a victory in faith by not being stained with sin and evil.

Steadfast Spirit

"Create in me a clean heart,
   O God, and renew a steadfast spirit within me."
(Psalm 51:10)

The changeable heart is the heart that changes from what you planned to do or had set your heart to do originally. We change because we seek our own benefits or advantage. We often change our plans according to greed for money, fame, or authority. When we seek after only our personal benefits we sway from left to right. Those who don't keep their hearts and change easily cannot gain trust from anyone. If you change from your beliefs as a Christian you will not even receive salvation. The Bible tells us to *"watch over your heart with all diligence, for from it flow the springs of life"* (Proverbs 4:23). Therefore, we have to strive to have the unchangeable heart and steadfast spirit.

His Gentle Touch

"You who fear the LORD, trust in the LORD;
  He is their help and their shield."
(Psalm 115:11)

When I went to theological seminary, I lived
alone in a small house near my family's home.
At that time, my children were very little and
my wife and I were running a shop. After the
Dawn Service, I worked in the shop until late
in the afternoon, studied in the seminary,
offered prayer at night, and studied more
after the prayer. Then, I slept for around two
hours. It was during this time I heard a voice
saying 'Daddy!' from outside my door. But
when I went out, nobody was there. I looked
at the clock and realized it was time to get
up. After I experienced something similar
a few times, I came to realize God woke me
up. Such a gentle touch of God, it is always
around us. He always wants to help those
who believe and rely on Him.

The Power of Love

"We have come to know and have believed the love
which God has for us. God is love, and the one who abides
in love abides in God, and God abides in him."
(1 John 4:16)

Love makes seemingly impossible things
possible. That's why we say that love is so
powerful. The love of God towards men of
faith in particular is really amazing. He has
let them experience wonderful things which
are worthy of being written as touching
novels or produced as movies. The love of
God changes people who can't do anything
into those who can do anything. It changes
weakness into strength and poverty into
wealth. When His hand of love touches
people who were once foolish and arrogant,
they become wise and humble. Those who
seek God diligently can find God. In His
great love, we can be born again as the most
beautiful and precious of beings.

Just As You Have Compassion on the Plant

"Keep yourselves in the love of God,
   waiting anxiously for the mercy of our Lord Jesus Christ to eternal life."
(Jude 1:21)

According to the Bible, God sent Jonah, the prophet, to Nineveh because their wickedness had 'come up before God.' God had sent Jonah to warn them about His judgment. But Jonah wanted the city of Nineveh, which was the enemy of his people, to fall. So, when he saw the city repent and receive forgiveness, Jonah became angry. He made a shelter for himself and watched what was happening in the city. At that time, God put a plant over Jonah and it grew up to provide shade for Jonah. He was extremely happy about the plant. But next day a worm attacked the plant and it withered. Then, Jonah said, "Death is better to me than life." At that time, God gave him realization saying that it was natural for Him to have compassion on the people of Nineveh just as Jonah had compassion for the plant during the night. We should thankfully realize that it is by the great love of God that we could be forgiven of many sins and take the way of salvation and blessing.

Diligent Life

"Also righteousness will be the belt about His loins,
and faithfulness the belt about His waist."

(Isaiah 11:5)

The great figures in the Bible had not only
good faith, but they also led diligent lives.
For instance, David guarded his sheep from
the attacks of lions or bears even putting his
life at risk. Shepherding the flock alone in
the fields might not have been that fun a job
for a boy with strong curiosity. Nevertheless,
he fulfilled his duties and established the
foundation of his life diligently. In the end,
he came to rule over not sheep but all the
sons of Israel. What is your duty? I hope you
will realize that doing your best in all your
works now will serve as the firm foundation
to achieve all your future goals.

The Words that We Must Heed

"The angel of the LORD encamps around those who fear Him,
and rescues them."

(Psalm 34:7)

Ahab, king of Israel assembled prophets to examine God's will before he attacked Aram. Around 400 false prophets prophesied that he would win the battle, but only one prophet, Micaiah, delivered the true Word of God and prophesied he would lose the battle. But Ahab was full of greed to occupy the land by winning the battle at that time. So the king ignored Micaiah's words and waged war. In the end, he died in the battle. Therefore, we have to pay heed not to what agrees with man, but with the will and the Word of God alone. Only in His will and Word can we lead a prosperous and blessed life.

The Lie of Sarah

"Behold, You desire truth in the innermost being,
and in the hidden part You will make me know wisdom."
(Psalm 51:6)

One day God told Abram that he would have a son at the age of 100. At that moment his wife Sarah heard it too, and laughed inside with unbelief. She whispered to herself, "After I have become old, shall I have pleasure, my lord being old also?" God knew she had laughed and asked her why she had laughed. She was surprised and denied it saying that she didn't laugh. Like Sarah, if we are not honest in our hearts then we are not able to realize it when we do lie. We also will lose the chances to change when we try to hide our shortcomings and faults. Those who are honest can always speak good words and show good behavior all the time.

The Boomerang of Judgment

"Do not judge so that you will not be judged.
For in the way you judge, you will be judged;
and by your standard of measure, it will be measured to you."
(Matthew 7:1-2)

Judgment is discerning good from bad, or right from wrong. People usually pass judgment on those who are seemingly doing something wrong. So nobody likes to be judged. Those who do pass judgment on others seemingly think that in comparison they are beyond being judged by others. Such judgment passed on others is like a boomerang that returns to the one who passed it. Also, in this verse the 'measure' represents the standard of discerning what happened. In other words, it is assuming things thinking "he might have done this or that" and even though the truth actually is not known, they are sure they are right. However, when an individual does use a personal measure, most of these measurements are not true and it will return to him like a boomerang.

Wisdom of Waiting Quietly

"But refuse foolish and ignorant speculations,
 knowing that they produce quarrels."
(2 Timothy 2:23)

Sometimes you may be misunderstood because of something you failed to say or something you didn't do. Other times, even out of good intention, something you do or say may be misinterpreted. At times others may speak ill of you or make up a false story involving you. If you are in such a situation, don't argue about what is right or wrong, but just keep quiet. The more you make excuses, the more false rumors can be spread. It is not good to argue if you have to reveal others' faults to resolve a misunderstanding. You might as well keep quiet and shelter others from harm. When they know your heart and situation, their hearts will be melted and they will seek to establish a stronger relationship with you.

The Great Man and the Small Man

"Let another praise you, and not your own mouth;
a stranger, and not your own lips."
(Proverbs 27:2)

Great men give credit to others when they are praised. They even feel embarrassed when they get special treatment. Such a heart is the heart of goodness. On the other hand, small men want to be praised after achieving a tiny thing. But they don't like it when others are acknowledged for something good. Good-hearted men don't want to argue about what is right or wrong. They don't store up evil or make record of other bad points. God, who is goodness itself, is looking for men who are good-hearted and have great heart-vessels and lead them to the way of blessing.

Wise Reproofs

"For the commandment is a lamp and the teaching is light;
and reproofs for discipline are the way of life."
(Proverbs 6:23)

Before you find it necessary to point out
someone's wrongdoing or rebuke him, it is
effective to compliment his good points first.
You can say, "You are really good at this. But,
why don't you try to change that a little?"
In this way he will be more open to you and
admit his shortcoming in a positive way. If he
doesn't deserve any praise, you might as well
not reprimand him at all because he may only
feel more discouraged about doing nothing
praiseworthy. He may lose heart or even fall
into despair when facing only reprimand.
In such a case it will be both wise and good
to give prudent advice with love rather than
reprimand or rebuke.

To Utter Beautiful Words

"For my mouth will utter truth;
and wickedness is an abomination to my lips."
(Proverbs 8:7)

We utter many words every day. There are bad words that hurt others' feeling as well as positive and beautiful words. Sometimes a word can change the direction of life. Words come from thoughts and thoughts come from the heart. Therefore, it's not easy to speak good words if you don't get rid of the evil in your hearts. This is because things in the heart come out on the lips. Figuratively speaking, peaches are sweet and lemons are sour although both of the trees are rooted in the same ground. That is, they can't but give what they bear. Thus, we must keep in mind that the most important thing is that we have to become sanctified by living in the Word of God.

The Heart of Goodness

"Above all, keep fervent in your love for one another,
because love covers a multitude of sins."

(1 Peter 4:8)

There are people in the world who are hurt
or suffer deeply because of rumors. If it is a
false rumor, it will be even more deadly. After
Mary was betrothed to Joseph, she was found
to be with child before they came together.
But Joseph planned to send her away secretly
though he actually could have stoned her to
death. Even though Joseph didn't know Mary
carried a child by the Holy Spirit, he didn't
want to make it known to others. Since he
had such a good heart God let Joseph bring
up the baby Jesus. God, who embraces us
with unlimited love and forgiveness, also
doesn't want us to pass judgment carelessly
nor spread others' faults. He wants us to lead
a life of love and forgiveness.

The Merciful Man

"The merciful man does himself good,
but the cruel man does himself harm."
(Proverbs 11:17)

A merciful man usually sees others' strengths, not weaknesses. He doesn't see other's shortcomings, but just remembers what they did well, forgives their faults, and offers another opportunity to succeed. He doesn't have any arguments with anyone and his life itself stays at peace. Even if he is falsely accused of some wrongdoings his acquaintances and friends will protect him by proving his innocence saying, "He is not that kind of person." Therefore, I hope you will become a merciful man in your life and enjoy peace all the time.

Active Goodness

"Let love be without hypocrisy.
 Abhor what is evil; cling to what is good."
(Romans 12:9)

Suppose your child is worried after he spills food on the expensive carpet at home. Then, if you say, "It's OK," he will become more relaxed and thankful to you just because he isn't reprimanded or punished. In addition, if you say with a cheerful voice, "I was about to wash the carpet. So I can do now." How do you think the child would feel? He would not only become relaxed but also feel the tenderness and mercy of your heart. Moreover, he will keep it in mind so that it does not happen again. It is in this way that active goodness goes beyond just forgiveness and can move others' hearts and work more effectively than any reproofs. It will also serve as a driving force for them to change and improve.

Having Inner Beauty

"Who is like the wise man and who knows the interpretation of a matter?
A man's wisdom illumines him and causes his stern face to beam."
(Ecclesiastes 8:1)

These days, people pay extreme attention to their appearances regardless of sex. But what is more important than their appearance is their inner hearts. Nobody raises a question against it. To make our hearts beautiful we have to live in the Word of God who is truth itself. To the extent that our heart is cultivated with truth, blessing and external beauty follow. An evil-looking face will change into gentle-looking face. Even faces darkened with anxiety and worries will glow with spiritual light. Ordinary-looking men will look better and attractive. They will naturally garner the attention of others.

Barzillai's Serving

"But you, be strong and do not lose courage,
for there is reward for your work."

(2 Chronicles 15:7)

David, the great king of Israel had to flee from his palace due to the rebellion of his son, Absalom. He met a man named Barzillai on the way. He served the king David and the people with him, who had no food and no shelter, with all his heart. After the rebellion was suppressed David asked Barzillai to go and reside at his palace, but he turned him down politely. It might have been an opportunity to enjoy wealth, fame, and glory because David again governed Israel. But, he rejected it since he was now old and didn't want to be a burden to the king. It showed that Barzillai had served David with no desire for personal reward. Many people change their minds considering the benefit or loss to them. But Barzillai's actions let us realize what a true Christian should be like.

The Principle of Priming the Pump with Water

"Many will seek the favor of a generous man,
 and every man is a friend to him who gives gifts."
(Proverbs 19:6)

When you use a pump to get water from underground, you need a bowl of water. This water is called priming water. Namely, we need to prime the pump with a bowl of water to gain a great deal of water. Those who seek their own benefit and don't share with others might enjoy wealth, but their hearts become hardened and one by one people leave them. However, when we are considerate of others and share things with them, our lives will be abundant and we will gain many people just as priming water leads to a lot of water. And this is why Acts 20:35 tells us, *"It is more blessed to give than to receive."*

Good Feeling

"Let your light shine before men in such a way
that they may see your good works,
and glorify your Father who is in heaven."

(Matthew 5:16)

Some say they can't help but feel bad seeing
a person they hate even if they try to cast
away such hard-feelings. But feelings depend
on thought. Even if you see a good-hearted
man, if you think you hate him, you feel bad
and hold hard feelings against him. Even if
you encounter a man whose way of thinking
doesn't agree with yours, you can feel good
about it when you understand him from
his position. Also those who think violence
in a movie is exciting can become a violent
person. If they think, 'Violence gives others
hard time. I will never do it,' they can become
gentle men. If we think in goodness like this
and accept everything with good feelings, our
hearts will resemble God's heart which is love
and goodness.

Enjoy Waiting

"Therefore I say to you, all things for which you pray and ask,
  believe that you have received them, and they will be granted you."
(Mark 11:24)

Some people make mistakes because they act impulsively. They always do something quickly. But there are times when we have to wait patiently and at ease. God promised Abraham to multiply his descendants as the 'stars of the heavens.' But it took a long time for him to gain the first son. Abraham, however, didn't doubt at all. He finally gained Isaac, his son, at the age of 100. The twelve tribes of Israel were formed through Jacob, Isaac's son. Abraham also was acknowledged as the 'father of faith' and gained countless descendants of faith. God's Word is fulfilled absolutely and all the time. Many Christians want to receive answers quickly, but the God of love answers our prayers at the best time.

"Then God said, 'Let the waters below the heavens be gathered into one place, and let the dry land appear'; and it was so. God called the dry land earth, and the gathering of the waters He called seas; and God saw that it was good."

Genesis 1:9-10

The Vitality of Earth

"Thus says God the LORD, who created the heavens
  and stretched them out, who spread out the earth and its offspring,
  who gives breath to the people on it and spirit to those who walk in it."
(Isaiah 42:5)

People say that the earth is alive because when we plant seeds in the earth the seeds sprout and their fruit is borne. This is the evidence that the earth is living although the earth has no respiratory apparatus. Its vitality positively influences people as they breathe while their steps make contact with the earth. That's why some have health problems when they live in places with no bare earth for a long time. Then, what makes the earth so mysterious? It was God the Creator who gave the earth the ability to sustain living creatures when He created the Earth.

All Things Came into Being through the Creator

"The earth brought forth vegetation, plants yielding seed after their kind,
and trees bearing fruit with seed in them, after their kind;
and God saw that it was good."
(Genesis 1:12)

Plants can survive only when they are provided with sunshine and water. The Bible tells us that when God was creating the heavens and the earth and all things in them, God created plants before He created the sun. Furthermore, there was water in the sea, but there was no water on the earth because it hadn't rained yet. Then, why did God create plants even before the sun and water to sustain them? This is because God wanted to let us, mankind, know it is God's power that allowed for even a blade of grass to grow and a flower to blossom. The whole universe didn't just appear by coincidence nor does it exist by itself. It is under the control of God the Creator.

Mysterious Power

"And he began reasoning to himself, saying,
'What shall I do, since I have no place to store my crops?'"
(Luke 12:27)

Each flower blossoms on time and in a certain order every year as if someone told them, "Golden-bells, blossom first. Cherry-blossoms, you're next. Then the magnolia and rose, you are the next." They bloom according to the order at the right time. Spring flowers come out during the period when day is longer than night. Autumn flowers blossom during the period when night is longer than day. Such a mysterious power was given to them by God when they were created in the first place. Plants and flowers conform to the providence of Creation, come into bloom, and show their beauty at the right time.

The Wisdom of the Creator

"All things came into being through Him,
  and apart from Him nothing came into being that has come into being."
(John 1:3)

Closely observing plants, you might think they are very mysterious. If their seeds were to fall down around the parent flowers, they would grow together in a small place and lack water and nutrients. Thus, it's beneficial for them to be scattered out far from each other. God knew this and let plants spread their seeds in the most effective ways. For example, God made a 'device' that works like a parachute for dandelion seeds so that they can fly to far-distant places. Balsam seeds are devised to scatter about in all directions when their seed bags burst. Some seeds are given to birds or animals as their food. The animals carry the seeds and spread them. Seeing all these things, how can we help but be amazed by the wisdom of God the Creator!

The Love Embedded in a Blade of Grass

"Then God said, 'Behold, I have given you every plant yielding seed that is on the surface of all the earth, and every tree which has fruit yielding seed; it shall be food for you."
(Genesis 1:29)

Some spring herbs like certain stone crop, mugwort, shepherd's purse stimulate appetite. These days, our environment has been polluted by chemicals and chemical fertilizer that people use out of greed. But the herbs growing in the mountains and the field are alkaline food that is good for our health because they have plenty of vitamins and minerals. Before God created us, He created plants yielding seed and fruit trees to give their fruits to us. When we open our hearts a little bit, we can feel the love of God just seeing a blade of grass.

The Well that Never Runs Dry

"But whoever drinks of the water that I will give him shall never thirst;
 but the water that I will give him will become in him
 a well of water springing up to eternal life."
(John 4:14)

The fields become dry due to long periods
of drought. But, if it finally rains after a
long wait, mountains, valleys, flowers, and
trees will be full of energy. It applies to our
spirits as well. Until we are filled with God's
Word, which is a well where the water never
becomes dry forever, we will feel thirst and
emptiness that nothing else can satisfy. Since
human nature has longing for eternity, it's
not until men meet God the Creator that
they realize the true meaning of life. Then,
they will feel satisfied in spirit. When we
seek God diligently and live according to His
will, God takes care of us and becomes the
fountain of water that never runs dry.

The Seeds and the Fruit of Words

"Words from the mouth of a wise man are gracious,
while the lips of a fool consume him."
(Ecclesiastes 10:12)

When we sow pumpkin seeds, pumpkins grow. When we sow apple seeds, apples are borne. In much the same way, the result will be different according to what kinds of words we 'sow'. Gideon, a judge of Israel, achieved a landslide victory by the help of God, but there were some people who were furious about Gideon not calling them when he fought. Gideon didn't confront them but humbled himself and complimented their past achievement saying, "What have I done now in comparison with you?" Such seeds of good words turn into the fruit of peace.

What We Must Not Forget

"A man's pride will bring him low,
  but a humble spirit will obtain honor."
(Proverbs 29:23)

A saying goes, "It is an old cow's notion that she was never a calf." We use this saying when someone who used to have times of difficulty brags about what is now possessed, without remembering the past hardships. There was this kind of person in the Bible. It was Saul. When he was chosen as a king of Israel he was such a humble man that he hid himself out of shyness. But he became arrogant after taking the throne and even disobeyed the will of God. In the end, he was forsaken by God. Is there anyone who has developed a lofty heart like Saul just because he or she has been a Christian for a long time or his or her business is booming? We should remain humble by engraving in our hearts the Bible verse saying, *"Therefore let him who thinks he stands take heed that he does not fall"* (1 Corinthians 10:12).

Jesus' Method

"I planted, Apollos watered,
  but God was causing the growth."
(1 Corinthians 3:6)

Jesus' disciples had different jobs. Some
were fishermen and one was a tax collector.
At times they couldn't understand Jesus'
Words nor could they grow in faith. They
had deficiencies and shortcomings. But
Jesus saw their good points like their efforts,
their hearts, and their love. Jesus led them
to fulfill their God-given duties by receiving
consolation and strength from God.
Likewise, if we want to help others grow up
in faith, we must not just point out their
wrongdoings and reprimand them, but we
must encourage them and wait for them to
change with hope.

Accumulated Strength

"Again I say to you, that if two of you agree on earth
  about anything that they may ask, it shall be done for them
  by My Father who is in heaven."
(Matthew 18:19)

A snowflake is too light for us to feel its
weight. When snowflakes are piled up
however, branches are broken or become
bent. Sometimes they cause massive
avalanches. In the same manner, a mere
thought, a word, or an action accumulate
in our daily lives. They end up having
tremendous impact on our lives. One person's
strength seems very weak, but the strength of
many can be exerted with astounding power.
So we must not say, "It's just a trivial thing"
or "It's just me, how can I do anything." We
must have a heart saying, "It's a big deal" or
"It's I who has to do so."

True Friends

"Take hold of instruction; do not let go.
 Guard her, for she is your life."
(Proverbs 4:13)

No matter how close you are to your friend, it's not easy to reprimand him. This is because his feelings can be hurt and you might get stuck in an unfavorable situation because of your reprimand. Therefore, only when you have sacrificial love with which you want him to be better-off can you reprimand him effectively. When David, the king of Israel, committed sins before God, Nathan the prophet rebuked him. David repented immediately and received forgiveness from God and recovered the grace of God. When reproof is necessary instead of fine-sounding words, it is in this way that we can be true friends with love. This is true love.

Think in Goodness

"A good man will obtain favor from the LORD,
 but He will condemn a man who devises evil."
(Proverbs 12:2)

People can be different according to the kinds of thoughts they have in the same situation. Let's say two people are whispering to each other and giggling. Then, if you think, "They're really irritating me," you will feel uncomfortable every time you are in a similar situation. However, if you just think "They have something to talk about quietly," you will think like that whenever you see people whispering. The situation is the same but the response is totally different. We should know God blesses good-hearted people. Therefore, we have to make a habit of seeing and thinking in goodness.

Abraham's Wisdom

"To do righteousness and justice is desired
   by the LORD more than sacrifice."
(Proverbs 21:3)

People usually love things that are free-of-
charge, and have curious interest in free stuff.
What about Abraham, a role model for
Christians? He wanted to bury his dead wife
in the cave of Machpelah. The sons of Heth
who dwelled in the area and the landowner,
Ephron wanted to give the land to Abraham
for free. But Abraham paid a full price of
it since he had no selfish-motives. This was
because he knew the changing hearts of men.
So, by his actions he got rid of any source of
argument. We have to keep it in our mind
that there is no more expensive thing than
things we get for free. Let's have the wisdom
of Abraham.

To Exercise Self-control

"Everyone who competes in the games exercises self-control in all things. They then do it to receive a perishable wreath, but we an imperishable." (1 Corinthians 9:25)

Self-control is the ability to control one's own emotions, behavior and desires so as not to go beyond limits. Those who can't control themselves complicate their lives and cause major difficulties for themselves and others. For example, they could damage their stomach by overeating, or beat up others if they don't control their emotions. To maintain self-control we need to achieve unchanging hearts first. This is because when we cultivate our hearts into an unchanging and honest heart that has no attribute of a lying heart and a crafty heart, then strength to fulfill what we decide to do will come upon us. Of course, we cannot accomplish such a heart overnight. We have to practice guarding our hearts even doing things that are trivial. As long as you are determined to do something, you must not change your plan. When such efforts are piled up you will be able to exercise self-control.

When You Become Afraid
of the Storm

"Fixing our eyes on Jesus, the author and perfecter of faith..."
(Hebrews 12:2)

When Peter saw Jesus walk on the sea, he
asked Him to command him to come to
Him on the water. Peter got out of the boat
according to Jesus' command and walked on
the water. But seeing the wind, he became
frightened, and began to sink. When we act
in faith keeping our eyes fixed on Jesus, we
can show amazing works beyond human
capability and environmental limitations. But
when we fix our eyes on the problems before
us, faith departs and we just feel frustrated.
Sunflowers that fix themselves on the sun
look like the sun. In the same manner, those
who see only Jesus resemble Him and lead a
beautiful life like Him.

Knowing Trees by Their Fruits

"You will know them by their fruits.
 Grapes are not gathered from thorn bushes nor figs
 from thistles, are they?"
(Matthew 7:16)

We can tell that this is a grape tree and that is
an apple tree by seeing their fruits. Although
it's difficult just by seeing leaves, branches and
trunk, we can clearly distinguish trees when
we see their fruit. It's the same with humans.
Whether they are of evilness or goodness, or
whether they have faith or not, we can know
the person, by seeing their fruits. No matter
how properly a person may act demonstrating
manners and etiquette, the fruits of goodness
cannot be borne with a deceiving heart.

Acacia Wood's Story

"For he will be like a tree planted by the water, that extends its roots
 by a stream and will not fear when the heat comes; but its leaves will be green,
 and it will not be anxious in a year of drought nor cease to yield fruit."
(Jeremiah 17:8)

Acacia trees in the wilderness in Israel look
ugly because they grow in such a barren
environment, but they are very strong.
They grow strong by putting down a tap
root tens of meters under the ground to
keep alive. God had the Israelites make the
Ark of the Covenant with the wood of the
acacia tree and then layered it with gold. He
also had them put the two tablets of Ten
Commandments in the ark and place it in
the sanctuary. The tree was also used to build
the tent at that time. Likewise, those who
put down roots deep in the Word of God,
even under difficult situations, will be able to
lead a life of value on account of firm faith.
They will also be used in a way to accomplish
things that are precious.

Like Well-ripened Grapes

"Equip you in every good thing to do His will,
working in us that which is pleasing in His sight,
through Jesus Christ, to whom be the glory forever and ever."
(Hebrews 13:21)

Grapes grow ripe in the following sequence
of steps: flowers blossom and fall, and then
small grapes come out, grow larger, and they
become purple-colored over time. Even in the
same bunch, some grapes look more green-
colored, others are small, and still others
are purple-colored and big. Likewise, some
people have much love but lack self-control.
Others are decisive but lack gentleness. Just
as a bunch of grapes can become the best
product only when all of its grapes grow and
ripen well, we as humans can have a beautiful
character only when we cultivate all of the
good attributes including love, gentleness,
peace, and self-control.

Sweet Rain of Grace

"And Jesus said to him, 'If You can?'
 All things are possible to him who believes."
(Mark 9:23)

If a farmer pulls weeds in the rows of his field after it rains, he can easily pull them out without using a hoe. When he digs he fills and smoothes over the ground to level it. He can do it more easily after it rains because the ground is wet and soft. It's the same with our lives. Even if we are faced with problems that seem difficult to solve, we can solve it in but a moment when God gives us His grace. This is because God is almighty. He can solve problems that are impossible with human ability and lead us in the ways of prosperity.

Blessing of Thanksgiving

"Always giving thanks for all things
 in the name of our Lord Jesus Christ to God, even the Father."
(Ephesians 5:20)

In the past, my wife and I ran a small bookstore. One day, after I came back from mountain prayer, I heard some thieves had broken into the store and stolen many books. I thought to myself from the bottom of my heart, "God, thank You for removing old books." Afterwards, we got a phone call saying that a policeman caught the thieves. They were high school students. Their parents asked for favor in managing the situation. They wanted to compensate us for the books but we declined. Being moved by our acts of goodness, they even came to believe in God. Could we have experienced such a work of God if I had lamented saying, "How could such a thing happen to me when I have fasted and prayed?" By the same token, we can receive overflowing blessing prepared for us when we believe everything is in God's will, rejoice, and give thanks even in difficult situations.

An Appointed Time for Fruit

"There is an appointed time for everything.
And there is a time for every event under heaven."
(Ecclesiastes 3:1)

Until most blossoms on other trees have bloomed and withered in spring, no leaves come out on jujube tree. It blossoms late. Instead of the short early bloom, it blooms throughout the summer and shows off abundant fruit. In the same way, even if our efforts don't bloom right away and they have not yet borne fruit, we don't have to be disheartened. This is because the appointed time is different for the different fruit to be borne and you can bear much more fruit at the right time.

Everlasting Rewards

"Behold, I am coming quickly, and My reward is with Me,
to render to every man according to what he has done."
(Revelation 22:12)

What if people were to be given just one day
and told that they would receive gold according
to the number of stones they collected the very
next day? They would probably start at 12 A.M.
and diligently collect stones even until the very
last second of the day. They would cancel other
schedules and even want to save meal times and
break times as they work against the clock to
continue gathering. This is because their wealth will
be decided in accordance with how much they work
for that one day. It's the same with the heavenly
rewards. Eternal rewards will be decided according
to what kind of life we live until God calls our spirit.
Those who have such a hope for heavenly rewards
live working against the clock and don't hesitate to
preach the gospel of love.

God's Viewpoint

"All the ways of a man are clean in his own sight,
  but the LORD weighs the motives."
(Proverbs 16:2)

Nobel regarded himself as a person who made a great contribution to human history by inventing dynamite. But others thought of him as 'the merchant of death.' Knowing this, he was greatly shocked. How you regard yourself might be totally different as viewed by others. If you check yourself from the view-points of others it can be helpful to discover yourself. The most important point-of-view is how God views us. God, who searches the heart, acknowledges those who don't insist their ego but pursue peace with everybody.

The Heart of Love

"Love does no wrong to a neighbor;
  therefore love is the fulfillment of the law."
(Romans 13:10)

It's cloudy outside. A husband tells his wife to carry an umbrella when she is heading out. She doesn't pay attention to his advice. She ends up getting soaked in the rain and catching a terrible cold. Many husbands in the case might say, "I told you so, but you didn't listen to me." But if husband really loves his wife, he might be concerned about her condition first before blaming her. Of course, we need to discern between right and wrong, but it's more important to understand others and be considerate of their feelings. That's the heart of love God wants us to have.

"God made the two great lights, the greater light to govern the day,
and the lesser light to govern the night; He made the stars also.
God placed them in the expanse of the heavens to give light on the earth,
and to govern the day and the night, and to separate the light from the darkness;
and God saw that it was good."

Genesis 1:16-18

Part 4

The Lamp in Our Life

The Moon and Stars

"God made the two great lights, the greater light to govern the day, and the lesser light to govern the night."
(Genesis 1:16)

God the Creator created not only the sun and the moon but also countless stars to give light to the earth at night. Thanks to the sun, it is bright during the day. At night, the moon and stars guide the way of men with their lights. Living a life on this earth, we sometimes enjoy a prosperous and bright life like the sun. On the other hand, when we are faced with hardships, we feel like we're walking in the dark of night. But those who believe in God the Creator, who created the moon of the night as well as the sun of the day, receive new strength to overcome the hardship. I hope you will enjoy a happy life by realizing the love of God through the moon shining and stars twinkling through the dark of night.

The Mystery of the Universe

"Lift up your eyes on high and see who has created these stars,
the One who leads forth their host by number,
He calls them all by name; because of the greatness of His might
and the strength of His power, not one of them is missing."
(Isaiah 40:26)

Countless stars, the planets, and their moons
in the universe have something in common.
All of them are globular in shape like a ball.
What about pebbles? Great rocks are broken
and become worn smooth by rain and wind.
At the river's bank and the sea's shore they
become pebbles and grains. However, they
are still not globular. Some are flat and round
and others are elongated. They are different
in shape even though their angles have been
worn smooth after thousands of years. But
countless stars including the sun and the
moon in the universe have the same shape;
all of them are globular like a ball. This is
because God the Creator designed them in
the shape that has perfect balance.

Let's Not Give Up Our Dream

"All the brothers of a poor man hate him;
  how much more do his friends abandon him!
  He pursues them with words, but they are gone."
(Proverbs 19:17)

Not long ago, a person donated millions of dollars to the poor, but he didn't want his name known as the benefactor by the public. He was called an anonymous angel. He started to help the poor because he couldn't forget his past life when he had lived in an old shack, which makes us imagine how hard his life was. Only those who have suffered from poverty know the poor man's heart. Only those who have suffered from diseases know the sick man's heart. They can wholeheartedly understand pain and sickness people suffer and have mercy on them. So you must not think you are unhappy when the reality is harsh. You have to think it makes you grow up and serves as a step to achieve your dream.

Until You Achieve Your Goal

"But He knows the way I take;
  when He has tried me, I shall come forth as gold."
(Job 23:10)

Successful men have a trait in common. It is their thorough preparation. Lincoln said, "If someone gives me six hours to cut a tree, I will use four hours to choose a good ax." It is important to set a goal, but it is also very important to prepare thoroughly to achieve the goal. The greater the goal, the more thorough the preparation should be. Preparation also needs perseverance. Just as athletes go through harsh training with perseverance to achieve a medal in the Olympics, only those who are well-prepared with diligence and patience under any circumstance will enjoy the joyful moment of achieving their goal.

The Secret to Gaining New Strength

"Yet those who wait for the LORD will gain new strength;
  they will mount up with wings like eagles, they will run and not get tired,
  they will walk and not become weary."
(Isaiah 40:31)

One night during a heavy snowstorm in the Alps, a man died because he was overcome by despair thinking he was lost. However, at that time he was just five meters from the cabin on the summit of the mountain. People set individual goals. Some want to pass exams and some others desire to succeed in their businesses. Christians want to enter beautiful Heaven. In the process to achieve the goal, there could be a storm-like hardship or severe sufferings. But, if you march with faith until the end, even in such hardships, God will pour down new strength upon you and there is absolutely no doubt that you will reach your destination.

With Your Beloved One

"For this is the love of God, that we keep His commandments;
and His commandments are not burdensome."
(1 John 5:3)

An advertisement company in the U.K. gave a quiz about the fastest way to get to London from Edinburgh, Scotland. There were many responses. Among them, a person said the fastest way is to go with the one who is our beloved. His answer was chosen and he received a great prize. If we are with our beloved one, we can travel to a faraway place with joy. It feels like a short trip. We are willing to do what our beloved asks no matter how difficult it may seem. Likewise, when we love God it's not difficult to live by His Word. In fact it's rather a source of happiness. God is with such people all the time and gives blessings of prosperity in all things.

The Most Precious Thing

"But now faith, hope, love, abide these three;
  but the greatest of these is love."
(1 Corinthians 13:13)

If you could take just one thing to Heaven, what would you take? King Alexander issued his final will asking them to let his hands show through two holes in his coffin. He wanted to show people he didn't take anything when he died! When we take the last breath, only our spirit and soul will go to Heaven. Even if we amass a lot of gold, silver, and jewels on the earth, they are useless in Heaven. But we can take one thing to Heaven and it is considered valuable there. It is love. We can possess true love to the extent that our hearts resemble the heart of Jesus Christ. Only such love is eternal and precious and the one thing we must strive to possess.

The Condition of Love

"If you address as Father the One
  who impartially judges according to each one's work,
  conduct yourselves in fear during the time of your stay on earth."
(1 Peter 1:17)

Some of you may think 'Why can't I be loved by others? Is it because I am not pretty enough or is it because I have nothing to boast about?' But all of the reasons like these are wrong. If people love you because of such external conditions, their love can't last for long. This is because their love will change when another person shows up seeming to be better. To receive unchanging true love, it is not the external conditions you have to change that are just skin deep, but you must change your spirit into a lovely one. In other words, we have to possess the heart of goodness with no evil. Such people move others' hearts and give out the fragrance of Christ. They are loved and praised by others.

To Make the Good Heart Shine

"You see that faith was working with his works,
  and as a result of the works, faith was perfected."
(James 2:22)

A saying goes, "Nothing is complete until you put it in its final form." It means even if there are so many good things, they become precious and valuable only when we organize them and make them useful. The same applies in God's works. To give out the light of the heart of goodness, it's important to act in goodness. For example, there is a big difference between just caring about the poor in your heart and giving them strength and sharing even small things with them. A small present and a warm word of consolation can make all the difference. Only when you give strength with good deeds following can the goodness in your heart truly shine and you can receive the love and blessings of God.

Let's Check Our Hearts

"Wash your heart from evil, O Jerusalem, that you may be saved.
How long will your wicked thoughts lodge within you?"
(Jeremiah 4:14)

Some people complain or feel jealousy when they see the unrighteous enjoy comfort and well-being. Their prosperous lives look good enough to agitate their hearts, or they may even consider that they too can succeed with such evil schemes. It is an evidence of their doubt in the justice of God who lets them reap what they have sown. It is also a proof that shows they have evil hearts. The hearts of jealousy and complaints can cause them to do the same evil things. Those who really live in God don't have any complaints or jealousy, so we have to check our Christian lives.

Discomfort

"And God is able to make all grace abound to you,
so that always having all sufficiency in everything,
you may have an abundance for every good deed."
(2 Corinthians 9:8)

When you don't get what you want, you might experience some discomfort. Those who do experience such discomfort tend to accuse others when they think those people should have yielded to them and should have given good things to them. It is recorded in the Bible that Abraham lived with his nephew Lot, but they had to live separately from each other at one point. At that time Abraham told Lot to choose the land first. He didn't feel discomfort when Lot chose the better land and left. Abraham was just good like that and because of it God gave him great blessings. If we could just come to see God and become true Christians, we would never have discomfort but instead we could always rejoice when others have good things.

A Soft Tongue Breaks the Bone

"By forbearance a ruler may be persuaded,
and a soft tongue breaks the bone."
(Proverbs 25:15)

Sometimes we are falsely accused. In such a
situation some people don't withhold their
anger but let it burst out. Then, from that
point the situation will just deteriorate.
Instead, it's better to wait calmly until people
stop talking and reveal the truth with a soft
voice. Then, your patience and soft words
will impress those around you and your
words will be more persuasive. It will lead you
to the way out of the false accusation. I hope
you will realize how strong soft words can be
and become a wise man who solves problems
with soft words.

True Strength

"And we know that the Son of God has come,
 and has given us understanding so that we may know Him who is true;
 and we are in Him who is true, in His Son Jesus Christ
 This is the true God and eternal life."
(1 John 5:20)

Jesus, who came to the earth to save us, manifested countless signs and wonders. He made the sea calm with a word and set the sick free from their diseases. But what those who met Him felt was His humbleness and service. He was always surrounded by many people. He was not able to eat nor sleep well. He served even a child. Jesus' deeds moved many people's hearts and allowed for them to come out as men of the truth. The strength that changes people doesn't come from great authority and dignity.

If God is with Us

"But God has chosen the foolish things of the world
to shame the wise, and God has chosen the weak things
of the world to shame the things which are strong."
(1 Corinthians 1:27)

God doesn't use people seeing their external
condition or ability. He doesn't care about
their wealth, knowledge, extroverted
character, or introverted personality. Before
I met God, I had been sick for a long time.
Peace in the family was broken and we had
accumulated huge debt. I couldn't have even
imagined I would become a pastor. But at
the moment I knelt down before God all my
diseases were healed and I regained happiness
in family. I cleared the debts in a short period
of time. I was called as God's servant and
became a pastor who preaches the gospel.
Even those who are weak can lead a valuable
life when God is with them.

The Reproof of Love

"He who rebukes a man will afterward find more favor
than he who flatters with the tongue."
(Proverbs 28:23)

People usually love being praised but don't like
being reprimanded. When someone rebukes them
to help them realize their faults, discomfort arises
from their hearts. Let's say you are on your way to
your destination but on the wrong road and people
traveling with you just compliment you on your
driving without letting you know you are on the
wrong path. Are you really grateful to them? You
may fall into difficulties because you mistakenly
think you are doing a good job but you are actually
not doing what you are supposed to do. It is only
then that you will realize nobody loves or cares
about you. On the other hand, if there is a person
who corrects your wrongdoings, you have to realize
his sincere love, believe him more earnestly, and
love him more.

Relenting of Evil

"And rend your heart and not your garments.
 Now return to the LORD your God,
 for He is gracious and compassionate,
 slow to anger, abounding in lovingkindness and relenting of evil."
(Joel 2:13)

Sometimes you think "Does God really forgive such an evil man?" But you say so because you don't know the heart of God who is love itself. The people of Nineveh received warning from Jonah the prophet of God because their evil was rampant. Jonah said that the city of Nineveh would be destroyed within 40 days. Actually, they couldn't be forgiven. But they repented and God forgave them. Even though people commit sins that can't be forgiven, if they thoroughly repent and turn away from their wrongdoings, God will have mercy on them. It is the heart of God.

No Difference?

"You shall thus observe My statutes and keep My judgments,
so as to carry them out, that you may live securely on the land."
(Leviticus 25:18)

There are some people who violate rules or break promises easily. They think it's not a big deal because they are just one individual among so many people and their action will not make any difference. There was such a person in the Bible who caused big trouble for all Israel because he thought that way. It was Achan. All the loots from the city of Jericho had to be given to God. But he violated the Word of God and hid an expensive mantle, gold, and silver in his tent. The nation of Israel had achieved victories without ceasing at that time, but they were brutally defeated at Ai because of the sin of one person, Achan. Only after Achan, who had sinned, was put to death, could the Israelites continue to win the battles. Therefore, we have to throw away such evil in our hearts and keep rules and promises all the time.

When Becoming
a Clean Glass Jar

"For it is sanctified by means of the word of God and prayer."
(1 Timothy 4:5)

There are times when we are moved by the words of others or learn lessons from what they say. Sometimes their words present the way of new life to us. In addition, amazing works of life take place in those who listen to the Word of God. But works will be different from person to person even though the word is the same. The holier preachers become, the greater the influence of the words on listeners is. When light passes through a clean glass jar, the light keeps its brightness. But when light passes through a glass jar stained with other substances the light is less bright. Only when we preach the Word with a pure heart with no spot and no blemish can the Holy Sprit's works of change take place.

When You are Faced with an Unfavorable Situation

"Do not say, 'I will repay evil';
  Wait for the LORD, and He will save you."
(Proverbs 20:22)

People usually tend to fight with others when they are falsely accused of something. But God wants us to do everything in goodness. Isaac, the son of Abraham, was faced with an unfair situation. At that time, a water well was like a lifeline because there was no abundant water. But some who felt jealous of Isaac filled in his well. They also took his wells by force a couple of times. Nevertheless, Isaac didn't fight against them. The Bible says that he was more greatly blessed and extended his lands even further. Likewise, if we pursue goodness and peace, even under unfavorable situations, it might seem to cause some immediate loss but the result will turn out to be blessing.

The Lever of Life

"Behold, I am the LORD, the God of all flesh;
 is anything too difficult for Me?"
 (Jeremiah 32:27)

With a leverage we can easily move objects
that are very heavy. How good it would be
if we could use a little leverage to lift up
serious life problems and get rid of them!
Surprisingly, we can have such a lever because
there is nothing impossible in God! Even
today those who live in the Word of God
written in the 66 books of the Bible can
experience the miracles in the Bible. I hope
you will enjoy having everything go well in
your lives all the time by getting the lever of
life in God the Almighty.

Broadening Hearts

"He who is slow to anger is better than the mighty,
 and he who rules his spirit, than he who captures a city."
(Proverbs 16:32)

When we put a spoonful of salt into a big pot filled with food, it doesn't make much of a change in the taste. But the same amount of salt in a very small pot makes the food very salty. The end result depends on the size of containers. People also vary in reaction according to the size of their heart vessels. Those who are broad-hearted hardly ever lose composure while those who are narrow-hearted can lose it over very small things. We have to broaden our hearts to harbor many people and accomplish great works. In order to do so, we need to think positively under any circumstance and train ourselves with goodness.

The Root of Blessing

"All Scripture is inspired by God and profitable for teaching,
for reproof, for correction, for training in righteousness."
(2 Timothy 3:16))

Today the standard of success tends toward great wealth and high position and authority. People focus on self-improvement to be better than others. They are trying hard to increase their wealth through all kinds of information. However, Christians should put the first priority on obeying the Word of God. This is because the root of blessings is God. To live in the Word and try hard to do our duties is the right attitude of life. During the birthday party of the first US president, George Washington, a guest asked his mother how she was able to raise him to become such a great man. She answered with confidence, "There is no special way. I just taught him to obey the Word of God unconditionally."

Only by Grace

"But God demonstrates His own love toward us,
  in that while we were yet sinners, Christ died for us."
(Romans 5:8)

Let's say someone committed a grave sin and was sentenced to death. He will be executed after one month passes. Even if he were to be given a fancy house, clothes, and all sorts of delicacies for the one month, chances are he would lead a horrible life from day to day that was void of any happiness. But what if his death penalty was canceled thanks to a special pardon? There would not be words to express his joy. Such grace has been given to us. After Adam, the ancestor of mankind, had sinned by eating from the tree of knowledge of good and evil, he and all his descendants were destined to Hell as a result of the sins. But the God of love gave His only begotten Son, Jesus for us, for all mankind, and He let His Son bear our sins through crucifixion. By this act, the gate of salvation was opened. How great God's grace is!

Through Him
who Strengthens Me

"I can do all things through Him who strengthens me."
(Philippians 4:13)

The mustard seed is as small as a point of a pen. When the seeds sprout and grow up, the tree reaches about three meters tall. It is really amazing. We can apply this story to our life. Peter, the biblical figure was an ordinary fisherman. But by following Jesus he became a great apostle and led countless people to the Lord. God can make a man who is like the small seed achieve great works just as the small seed becomes a grand tree. God receives glory through those who believe and rely on Him.

"Then God said, 'Let the waters teem with swarms of living creatures,
and let birds fly above the earth in the open expanse of the heavens.'
God created the great sea monsters and every living creature that moves,
with which the waters swarmed after their kind,
and every winged bird after its kind; and God saw that it was good."
Genesis 1:20-21

The Best Designer

The Outstanding Designer

"God created the great sea monsters and every living creature that moves,
with which the waters swarmed after their kind,
and every winged bird after its kind; and God saw that it was good."
(Genesis 1:21)

Seeing their feathers, wings, skeleton construction, respiratory system, alimentary system, heart, and circulatory system, birds are like an outstanding machine that is optimally designed with aviation technology and dynamics. Therefore, they can fly more efficiently than any of the man-made flying machines. According to marine engineers' research on ship's speed, center of gravity, and economy, the most appropriate ratio of a ship's length and breadth is the ratio in the length and breadth ratio of fish. Through this, we can tell everything was created according to the wise design of God the Creator.

Beautiful Voice and Wings

"For every house is built by someone,
 but the builder of all things is God."
(Hebrews 3:4)

The sounds of the birds are soft and clear and it makes listeners feel refreshed. They have wings that enable them to fly freely in the sky. Why is that? This is because God put certain capabilities in all creatures because He treasured each of them during His Creation. In other words, God gave beautiful voices to song birds to show His heart which delights in praise. He also gave them wings so that people can feel the existence of different dimensional worlds. When He created even a little bird, He put in it His heart and intention toward mankind. Isn't it natural to look up into the sky when the birds fly?

Patience

"For you have need of endurance,
 so that when you have done the will of God,
 you may receive what was promised."
(Hebrews 10:36)

A saying goes, "A man can turn an ax into a needle if he keeps grinding it." It implies that we can achieve everything when we try hard. How much time and effort would we have to put into making a needle from an ax? Some say, "Isn't it better to sell the ax and buy a bunch of needles with the money? Why would a person do such a thing anyway?" But there is the One who keeps patiently working hard for us like the man who makes a needle from an ax. It is our God. Since He loves us, He grinds our hearts that have become hardened with stubbornness and prejudice, which are like the iron of the ax. He grinds it over and over again and changes us into the beautiful men of the truth.

The Most Blessed Man

"But store up for yourselves treasures in heaven,
   where neither moth nor rust destroys,
   and where thieves do not break in or steal."
(Matthew 6:20)

In the worldly standard, the life of a sincere
Christian might look pitiful. Usually people
want to enjoy and make full use of what
they have. But Christians endure loss of
fame, property, family, and even their life
for Jesus Christ. What enables them to do
so? It is their hope for Heaven. If there were
no Heaven and our life ended on this earth,
Christians would be truly pitiful. But Heaven
surely exists and God remembers even a
single good deed of us and repays us heavenly
rewards. Therefore, Christians are the most
blessed people.

With Human Strength

"For God so loved the world, that He gave His only begotten Son,
that whoever believes in Him shall not perish, but have eternal life."
(John 3:16)

Even if a person is wealthy, has authority, has
good manners, and receives a good education,
all he has are just for life on the earth. Even
if people live in all kinds of luxury, it doesn't
mean their souls are saved and they can enter
the kingdom of heaven. Just as leopards can't
change their own spots, we can't solve the
problem of salvation for ourselves. God gives
His unconditional love and opened the way
of salvation. The way is Jesus Christ. When
you believe in Him and live in the Word
you can receive salvation and go the way of
eternal life.

The Way of Life

"Jesus said to him, 'I am the way, and the truth,
and the life; no one comes to the Father but through Me."
(John 14:6)

There are many paths to take and ways to follow in this world. There is the way of education that leads to knowledge and there is the way of wealth that places money as the only means to measure prosperity. But even if we are highly educated and possess enormous wealth, they can't give us true and eternal life. Morality and ethics are no different. Even though they are highly educated, they instinctively seek personal benefits and increasingly become stained with evil. Acquiring much knowledge doesn't necessarily mean going the right way. Nobody and nothing can solve mankind's problems of sin and death. Only Jesus Christ became the way leading to true and eternal life through His death on the cross for us.

Wisdom of Coming before Him

"How great is Your goodness, which You have stored up for those
who fear You, which You have wrought for those who take refuge in You,
before the sons of men!"
(Psalm 31:19)

I have seen a herd of gnus running across
a field on TV. When they spotted a lake,
they rushed to the lake and drank the water.
While they drank in haste and without
caution, they were grabbed by crocodiles.
They didn't see them deep in the water. They
were eaten by the crocodiles because they
were preoccupied with just drinking water.
It's the same with life. Worldly pleasure seems
to satisfy the desires of people's hearts at first,
but as they take in more they feel emptier. In
the end most of them fall into death-like pain
and suffering. The true satisfaction of life lies
in God. Thus, we must have the wisdom of
going to God with a humble heart.

Life and Death

"And inasmuch as it is appointed for men to die once and after this comes judgment..."
(Hebrews 9:27)

Wise people have a great interest in the question, "How can a person prepare well for death?" Some people who are suffering from a disease that can never be cured at all may think that an earlier death is more appropriate than to continue to live with it. Some others think it wise in preparation for death to forgive those whom they have hated during their life on Earth and receive a peaceful death. No matter how well one has prepared for death, however, what is the use of anything he has done under the sun unless he is able to gain salvation in the afterlife? Everyone must go either to Heaven or to Hell after his earthly life comes to a close. Those who have accepted Jesus Christ and lived by God's Word can go the path to Heaven, while those others who have not, must go the path to Hell. Please remember and act by the Scripture Ecclesiastes 12:1, which reads, "Remember also your Creator in the days of your youth, before the evil days come and the years draw near when you will say, 'I have no delight in them'" so that you may have no regret at the moment of death.

Keep as the Apple of Your Eye

"Keep my commandments and live,
  and my teaching as the apple of your eye."
(Proverbs 7:2)

It takes a fortieth second for a man to blink. When dust is about to get in to the eyes, eyelids quickly cover pupils. God always keeps an eye on His beloved children and protects them as the apple of His eye lest they are faced with disease, misfortune, or disaster. But in order to be protected by Him, we ourselves should keep the law of God as the apple of our eyes. If you think something is lawlessness you have to close the eyelid of your 'heart' so that you can live under God's secure protection.

The Lamb of God

"The next day he saw Jesus coming to him and said,
'Behold, the Lamb of God who takes away the sin of the world!'"
(John 1:29)

Some churches call newcomers 'lambs', but
we can see that the 'Lamb' refers only to
Jesus in the Bible. Among many animals on
the earth, a lamb is an animal that resembles
Jesus the most. A lamb is meek and gentle.
It doesn't hurt others nor resists even when
its wool is shaved. All it has—its wool, milk,
and even its flesh—is sacrificed in silence for
men. Likewise, Jesus gave His life on the cross
to redeem us from our sins and opened the
way of salvation wide for mankind.

To Become Rich

"All these blessings will come upon you
and overtake you if you obey the LORD your God."
(Deuteronomy 28:2)

In the past, a church member said, "I have no other choice but to be poor because I didn't receive a good education and I have nothing. But, still I am so thankful that I've received salvation and will go to Heaven." I told him, "That is like carrying a heavy burden in your arms while riding in a car because you are so grateful that you are being given a ride." Jesus is not only the way of salvation, but also He solved our problem of poverty by His living in poverty. Therefore, as believers you don't have to carry the burden of being poor. It is because anyone who lives in God's Word will be given blessing, so receive it!

Sufferings Do Good

"For if He causes grief, then He will have compassion according to
His abundant lovingkindness. For He does not afflict willingly
or grieve the sons of men."

(Lamentations of Jeremiah 3:32-33)

There are some sheep among the flock
that won't move but keep to themselves
in winter because they have a coat of wool
and eventually freeze to death. But if their
wool is sheared, the sheep move and brush
up against each other. By doing this they
become healthier. There are many examples
where people become stronger through trials
and lay the foundations of success. David, the
second king of Israel, relied on God while
he was avoiding King Saul who pursued him
to kill him out of jealousy and envy. David
broadened his heart and later became the
greatest of all kings of Israel by making the
nation prosper.

Difference between Jesus and Jesus Christ

"And there is salvation in no one else;
  for there is no other name under heaven
  that has been given among men by which we must be saved."
(Acts 4:12)

Those who have faith can experience God's works of answers and blessings. But some people pray just habitually 'in the name of Jesus' or 'in the name of Jesus Christ.' 'Jesus' means 'the One who will save His people from their sins.' It is a future form. On the other hand, 'Christ' is a Greek word that is translated as 'Messiah' in Hebrew. It means 'a Savior who has completed God's providence of salvation.' It is what is known as the non-continuous present perfect form for an action done in the past. Therefore, it is right to call the Lord 'Jesus' before He was crucified. After Jesus was resurrected we should call Him 'Jesus Christ', the Lord Jesus, or the Lord. We should pray in the name of the Lord Jesus Christ, which is spiritually correct.

Do Not Put off What You Can Do Today

"Behold, I stand at the door and knock; if anyone hears My voice and opens the door, I will come in to him and will dine with him, and he with Me."
(Revelation 3:20)

When Jesus was hung on the cross, a criminal who was hung next to Him received salvation by repenting just before death. He could be saved because he repented from the bottom of his heart at the last moment and believed in Jesus as his Savior. If he had been given another opportunity to live he wouldn't have lived the way he had lived. While preaching the gospel we come across some people who say "I will go to church later because I am just too busy now." or "I will go to church when I get older." But nobody knows what will happen even a split second from now. And those who are on the doorstep of death can't easily repent from their hearts. So you must not put off what you can do today. Accept Jesus Christ now when the door of salvation is opened wide. Live in the Word of God and be led to the heavenly kingdom safely.

True Repentance

"But if we walk in the Light as He Himself is in the Light,
we have fellowship with one another,
and the blood of Jesus His Son cleanses us from all sin."
(1 John 1:7)

God is full of mercy, gentleness, and love.
But, at the same time He is the God of justice
who lets people reap according to what they
have sown. He doesn't forgive or bless those
who live in sins. But He can forgive those
who repent and turn away from their sins.
Even if they sin, if they repent, God will
forgive with His unlimited love and solve
their problems in families, workplaces, and
also in health. But the repentance should be
a true one that God can accept. Suppose He
told you to go east, but you are going west.
You have to turn around and go east. That is
the true repentance and the way of blessing
that you can receive the love of God and His
mercy.

Let's Not Be Impatient

"A fool always loses his temper,
 but a wise man holds it back."
(Proverbs 29:11)

There are some people who burst out in their anger when they are faced with problems. Because of their quick-temperaments they complicate problems that are relatively easy to solve. Let's say such a person has mud on his shirt. He may try to get rid of the mud immediately. As a result, he gets other parts of the shirt muddy too. The better way is to wait a while for the mud to dry out a bit and dust the mud off. That is to say, as long as we control our impatience a little we can see solutions to our problems.

The Beauty of Forgiveness

"'Come now, and let us reason together,' says the LORD,
'Though your sins are as scarlet, they will be as white as snow;
though they are red like crimson, they will be like wool.'"
(Isaiah 1:18)

A woman had been caught in the act of adultery, in the very act. According to the Law, she was supposed to be stoned to death. But Jesus had pity on her as she trembled out of fear and He said, *"He who is without sin among you, let him be the first to throw a stone at her"* (John 8:7). Then, they had qualms of conscience and went away one by one. Finally, everybody left the place. Jesus forgave her saying, *"I do not condemn you, either. Go. From now on sin no more"* (John 8:11). Remembering the incident, it is doubtful that she committed any sin afterwards. We have to take after the love of Jesus and cast away judgment and condemnation, and have the heart of forgiveness.

True Freedom

"'...not by might nor by power, but by My Spirit,'
says the LORD of hosts."
(Zechariah 4:6)

Today many people are living in sins and
suffering because of hatred, jealousy, anger,
hot-tempers, and frustration. No matter how
hard they are trying to get out of it, they can't
escape with just their own strength. The
only One who can emancipate us from sins
is Jesus Christ. With His power, nothing is
impossible for us. If you want to be set free
from sins that are beyond your control, you
might as well believe in and rely on Jesus
Christ who is the way, truth, and life. There
are true freedom and peace only in Him.

Relying Only on God

"And do not neglect doing good and sharing,
 for with such sacrifices God is pleased."
(Hebrews 13:16)

I was deep in debt when I was so sick before I came to believe in God. After I met God and I was healed of all my diseases, I worked from early morning to late night with my wife. But most of my income was used to pay off the bank interest on my debt. It was hard to make ends meet. But I was trying to help those who didn't know God, the neglected and the poor. I was endeavoring to give charity and perform missionary works. I didn't hesitate to do it even when it meant that I wouldn't have anything to eat following day. Whenever I helped others and performed my ministry, God blessed my family in unexpected and wonderfully mysterious ways so that we had need of nothing. It led us to have greater faith with which we could rely only and completely on God.

The Law of Hope

"Now faith is the assurance of things hoped for,
the conviction of things not seen."
(Hebrews 11:1)

Flamingos in Jurong Bird Park, Singapore have the most beautiful light pink feathers in the world. They say that this is because the birds see light pink water and eat fish from the water. Through this, we can realize our appearance can be different according to what we see and take in. This is also supported by scientific data. Our hearts are much the same. What we see makes a difference. What we take in through our senses affects us. Our hearts can be changed into beautiful hearts or evil and filthy hearts depending on what we see and take in.

Do Goodness

"Do not fret because of evildoers, be not envious toward wrongdoers.
For they will wither quickly like the grass and fade like the green herb."
(Psalm 37:1-2)

Some evil men enjoy wealth, fame, and
authority in the world. Seeing them, some
other people complain saying, "How could
it happen if God is alive?" They seem
prosperous at first, but their glory disappears
over time just as grass withers. Even if they
enjoy prosperity, they will be judged by God
on the Day of Judgment. So we must not do
any unrighteous things during this time of
the earthly life, which flies like a moment. I
hope you will do good by relying on God and
enjoy praise and rewards in the eternity of
Heaven and enjoy earthly blessings as well.

The Life of Thanksgiving

"What shall I render to the LORD for all His benefits toward me?"
(Psalm 116:12)

It's natural to repay the grace of God when we receive it; however not many people do it nowadays. Even in the time of Jesus, ten lepers were healed by Jesus. Yet only one of them, the one from Samaria, came to give thanks to Him. Then, Jesus asked, "Where are the nine?" Then, He said, *"Stand up and go; your faith has made you well"* (Luke 17:19). He came before Jesus only to give thanks for healing him of his physical disease but Jesus proclaimed his salvation. By seeing this, we can tell how great a blessing it is in itself to give thanks for the grace of God!

Keys to Receiving Answers

"For He Himself is our peace, who made both groups into one and broke down the barrier of the dividing wall."

(Ephesians 2:14)

A man lives in the house where he can enjoy a beautiful sight overlooking a small river. One day, he discovered that the water had stopped flowing at some point upstream. He went to the upper region to figure out the reason. He found that someone had built a dam across it. When he destroyed the dam the water began to flow again. It's just a story, but it's the same with our walls between us and God. If we have walls of sins against God that are just like the dam, we cannot receive answers from Him until we destroy them. That's why we can enjoy an abundant life both in spirit and body, when we dwell in the 66 books of the Bible, because only then can the river of blessing flow freely.

The Best Happiness

"The second is like it, 'You shall love your neighbor as yourself.'
On these two commandments depend the whole Law and the Prophets."
(Matthew 22:39-40)

Have you ever given the most precious thing you possess to the one you love? The joy you feel when you share something is greater than any joy. Jesus, who is the Son of God, left all the heavenly glory behind and came to this lowly earth and was crucified to open the door of salvation to all mankind. He had the best love for mankind, so He could take the way He took with joy. It's difficult to give what is yours to those whom you hate, but it's never difficult to give even something precious to those whom you love. In fact, you feel rather happy with giving it. When you try hard to consider others before you think of yourself, you will get used to serving others and sharing things with them naturally. Such a life of love that loves neighbors like your own body will give you true happiness.

"Then God said, 'Let Us make man in Our image,
according to Our likeness; and let them rule over the fish of the sea
and over the birds of the sky and over the cattle and over all the earth,
and over every creeping thing that creeps on the earth.'"

Genesis 1:26

Beings that See Things Above

"Set your mind on the things above,
   not on the things that are on earth."
(Colossians 3:2)

'Anthropos' is from Greek and refers to man as 'beings that see things above.' It establishes a fundamental difference between animals and human beings. Animals consist of just body and soul, so they see only things on the earth and look for prey. But human beings are made of spirit, soul, and body, so when they see the sky they can envision Deity from within their nature. Animals return to the ground and soul ceases to exist when they die. But the spirit and soul of human beings have one of two ways to go after death. Those who accept Jesus Christ, have a reverent fear of God the Creator and live in goodness will go to Heaven, while those who see things on the earth just as the animals do will go to Hell.

The Reason God Created Man

"Then the LORD God formed man of dust from the ground,
 and breathed into his nostrils the breath of life;
 and man became a living being."
(Genesis 2:7)

Farmers plant apple trees with purpose of getting apples. Likewise, God also had a purpose in allowing for people to live on this earth. Although God had countless angels in Heaven, He wanted to gain true children with feeling and reason who would love God out of free will. It's just like though robots can be of great benefit to us, our children are much lovelier than robots. That's why God the Creator created man in His own image. He breathed the breath of life into his nostrils and allowed for him to dwell on the earth as a living being with free will.

Being that Created Me

"For You formed my inward parts;
  You wove me in my mother's womb."
(Psalm 139:13)

People often say that we got our bodies from our parents but our souls are given by God. However, our body and our organs are also given by God. Many want to choose the sex of their children and to have a healthy child. However, they have no control over the growing of so much as a single strand of hair on the head of their child. It is God the Creator who gives the sperm to a man and the egg to a woman. He also established the mechanism within them that produces all organs and passes the parents' dispositions such as personality, appearance, and habits to their offspring. That's why children resemble their parents in so many ways.

Go into Your Inner Room

"While I was fainting away, I remembered the LORD,
 and my prayer came to You, into Your holy temple."
(Jonah 2:7)

As medicine and technology have developed, the modern human life span has extended and the quality of life has improved. But still many people are suffering from emotional stress. Jesus says to them in Matthew 6:6, *"But you, when you pray, go into your inner room, close your door and pray to your Father who is in secret."* This means that you have to throw away idle thoughts in prayer just as you can cut yourself off from the world when you go into an inner room. It also means to pray to God from the bottom of the heart. Then, you can take a rest from the tedium of life in the world. You can enjoy an abundant life just as a tree firmly planted by streams of water yields its fruit in its season.

The Life that Never Crosses Line

"So you will walk in the way of good men
and keep to the paths of the righteous."
(Proverbs 2:20)

When Nehemiah rebuilt the walls of Jerusalem there were many people who tried to thwart his efforts. One day Shemaiah, an acquaintance, advised him to hide himself in the temple for they were coming to kill him that night. It was to frustrate Nehemiah's work and frighten him. It was also to cause him to enter the temple where only priests were allowed. But Nehemiah immediately said no, "Could one such as I go into the temple to save his life? I will not go in." He knew his position very well and didn't cross the line. By doing so, he preserved his life and achieved the dream of rebuilding the walls of Jerusalem. Likewise, when we know our position clearly and don't cross the line, we can bear good fruit.

Double-mindedness

"How blessed is the man to whom the LORD does not impute iniquity,
 and in whose spirit there is no deceit!"
(Psalm 32:2)

Sometimes a person can't decide what to eat when
he goes to a restaurant. He eventually chooses
something from among the many kinds of dishes.
But when he sees somebody else eating the selection
that he decided against, he regrets it thinking, 'I
should've ordered that to eat.' He would be happy
if he thought the dish he chose was the better
choice and just enjoyed it, but he continues to
think of the other dish, so he feels frustrated. If
you have such vacillating double-mindedness you
cannot be satisfied and happy. The same applies
when you ask something of God. When you have
double-mindedness between a believing heart and
a doubting heart you can't receive answers. Only
when you ask God with unchanging faith can you
receive the very best.

Trials and Growth

"And perseverance, proven character;
  and proven character, hope."
(Romans 5:4)

When a baby starts to take its first steps, his parents watch closely and put away things that could be dangerous. When the child is about to go a way that is dangerous they lead him in a safe way. God does the same thing for us. God allows us to undergo trials so that we can increase our faith, but He still protects us and guides us in the safest way. If you realize His love you will have more mature faith and understand the heart of God more deeply and give Him thanks from the bottom of your heart. Those who pray without ceasing, believe in God, and rely on Him can feel the warm love of God and do anything. Even though they sometimes have to go through major and minor ups and downs in their life's journey, it is still filled with joy and the warmth of His love.

If You Try Unchangingly

"Until we all attain to the unity of the faith,
and of the knowledge of the Son of God, to a mature man,
to the measure of the stature which belongs to the fullness of Christ."
(Ephesians 4:13)

When some people see others receive blessings, they just feel jealous thinking 'I want to have such faith.' They sometimes try, but become disappointed easily when they don't get what they want. But we should know that faith doesn't grow up all at once with a momentary effort. Just as those who don't usually read at all cannot suddenly become intelligent just because they read a dozen books over a couple of months, a person's faith cannot dramatically increase just because they try for a short period of time. But, just as knowledge is acquired over time, if you unchangingly try hard to live in the Word of God you can reach the level of mature faith. But the speed of maturing could be different according to the heart and the effort.

The Most Effective Way

"Do nothing from selfishness or empty conceit,
  but with humility of mind regard one another as more important
  than yourselves."
(Philippians 2:3)

One day, I wanted to use a computer but it didn't work. I tried to fix it, but it was of no use. I asked a person who knew about computers very well and he fixed it in a few minutes. If I hadn't asked him, I would have wasted a lot of time. In the same way, there are times when we are faced with situations where we need others' help. If a person insists on always doing everything for himself, he could really be slowed down and might miss a good opportunity to bear better fruit. Also, he easily breaks peace with others he has to work with. So when we set a goal and work toward it, we have to cast off selfish motives. We have to examine the most effective way and follow that way. This is the true wisdom.

Changing Love

"Beloved, let us love one another, for love is from God;
and everyone who loves is born of God and knows God."
(1 John 4:7)

King David had a son named Amnon. He loved Tamar who was his half sister so much that he was ill because of his unsatisfied love for her. In the end, he violated her and lay with her. After he satisfied his lust he came to hate her greatly and drove her out. It is the fleshly love, which changes over time even though it looks real at a glance. On the other hand, spiritual love doesn't change under any circumstance or condition. It always seeks the benefit of others. This is true love. Do you now see someone else's shortcomings even though you loved him/her at first? If you do, it means your love is fleshly love. So you have to check yourself all the time.

Something that Won't Disappear

"But certainly God has heard;
  He has given heed to the voice of my prayer."
(Psalm 66:19)

When I started to believe in God, I came to have new hope. Since I had experienced poverty and disease and hardship, I wanted to become an elder who receives great blessing and helps the poor and the sick. But not long after that God called me as the servant of the Lord. At first, I was confused and bewildered because I felt like all my prayers became nothing. But God gave me His power so that I could heal countless people both in spirit and body, and He blessed me to pastor a church that helps the poor and does His ministry. By doing so, I could achieve what I had prayed for even more greatly. I realized again that what we pray for to God diligently never disappears, but comes out as beautiful fruit.

Just As Jewelers Work on Jewels

"Counsel is mine and sound wisdom;
  I am understanding, power is mine."
(Proverbs 8:14)

No matter how precious a gemstone may be, it cannot display its beauty when still buried within a rock. But those who know the value dig it up and send it to a lapidary jeweler. After going through several steps of workmanship, the gemstone can give out beautiful light as fine jewel. God is like a jeweler that processes jewels. He carves corners and fills up shortcomings of one who is in His hands. He makes them vessels upon which He can pour out blessings. We have to believe in God the Almighty and commit our lives to Him. Then, you can enjoy a truly valuable life like a beautiful and precious jewel.

Clay and the Potter

"But now, O LORD, You are our Father, we are the clay,
 and You our potter; and all of us are the work of Your hand."
(Isaiah 64:8)

People think of many ways to achieve their goals. Some can achieve them, but others can't. It's different according to the size of their vessels. If you couldn't achieve a goal you should know that you don't have a vessel big enough to accomplish it. So you have to make your vessel bigger to achieve your goal. The way is in God the Creator who created men. When we as His creatures completely believe and rely on Him, He will make our vessels beautiful and use us as the most precious tool just as potters make vessels with clay.

Mysterious Power

"Be kind to one another, tender-hearted, forgiving each other,
just as God in Christ also has forgiven you."
(Ephesians 4:32)

Some who usually behave well act oddly
when they are faced with painful situations.
Most of them feel despair and anger. Peter
followed Jesus with love, but he denied Jesus
three times when Jesus was arrested. As Jesus'
greatest disciple, he had been loved by Jesus
so much. But, he denied Him before a life-
threatening situation. But Jesus understood
his weakness and forgave him, and He even
gave him new strength. Such love made
Peter able to preach the gospel and accept
crucifixion upside down as a martyr. Love
has power to change people. This mysterious
power makes people who are forgiven of sins
to have a great heart of forgiving faults and
wrongdoings of others.

Healthy Christians

"For even as the body is one and yet has many members, and all the members of the body, though they are many, are one body, so also is Christ."
(1 Corinthians 12:12)

Humbleness and service are a couple of the most important virtues that Christians should have. The passage saying "as the body is one yet has many members" puts an emphasis on these virtues. Suppose the eyes assumed that they are the most important of all parts of the body and ignored the functions of the lips, hands, and feet. What would happen? All the body members would fight against each other and the body wouldn't have peace and function well. Each member has different roles and all the roles are important. They can't say that their role is more important than any other. When all body members interact in their roles well, the body can become healthy. Only when we humble ourselves and serve others can we become 'healthy' Christians.

Warm Hands

"Give, and it will be given to you. They will pour into
 your lap a good measure pressed down, shaken together, and running over.
 For by your standard of measure it will be measured to you in return."
(Luke 6:38)

People think those who have many things
are happy. Some believe that when they
have money, fame, and authority they will
be leading a blessed life. So, many people
are trying hard to gain more and more. But
God loves men so much that He gave His
only begotten Son on the cross for them. He
gives everything to us so that we can know
the true joy of life. This is because we can
enjoy greater happiness when we take care of
the neglected and share what we have rather
than live in worries and anxiety to hold on to
what we have gained. God remembers a cup
of water that you've given to someone who
was thirsty and blesses you seeing your warm
heart and helping hands to neighbors. He
then can lead you to the way of blessings.

Driving Force of Success

"For since He Himself was tempted in that which He has suffered, He is able to come to the aid of those who are tempted."
(Hebrews 2:18)

Many people think when you grow your crops with no chemicals harmful insects will cause great damage. But it's not true. Rice that grows without any chemicals will grow well because it gains stronger vitality as it grows competing with harmful insects and the crop tends to grow better. When we meet people or an incident that looks like hurdles in your life, you might think you are likely to fail. In such a case you must not think, "If he hadn't been there..." or "If this hadn't happened to me..." But you must accept all the situations and overcome them with love. Then, this will become a driving force for success in your life.

You Must Not Give Up

"A battered reed He will not break off, and a smoldering wick
  He will not put out, until He leads justice to victory."
(Matthew 12:20)

When others do something wrong, some
good men keep patient and accept their
faults. But their acceptance has limitations
that they are willing to accept to varying
degrees. Even if the trouble maker is their
child, they sometimes just give up on them
when the problem is beyond a certain limit.
However, Jesus wanted to revive those who
have no possibility even if He couldn't help
but give them up. He knew Judas Iscariot
would betray Him but He taught him
everything and guided him until the end.
It is a perfect heart before God that loves
everyone with love and faith and never gives
him/her up.

We Need to Respect Everybody

"If you buy a Hebrew slave, he shall serve for six years;
  but on the seventh he shall go out as a free man without payment."
(Exodus 21:2)

In the past in Israel, Hebrew slaves were treated with a relative level of respect according to the God-given law. Even though they became slaves due to their unpaid debt, they were set free from the slavery when the appointed time came. After the emancipation, their masters had to help them live on their own by providing a flock, grain, and wine. We can feel the love of God who wanted them to respect, love, and cooperate with each other in the relations between subordinates and superiors, and between slaves and masters. We have to possess beautiful hearts that respect one another in any position of family and society, and give out true virtue and love.

Without It

"Pursue peace with all men, and the sanctification without which no one will see the Lord."
(Hebrews 12:14)

Jews want to be buried in the cemetery in the middle of Mount of Olives in Israel when they die. For them it is an honor and something hoped for because they regard the spot as the place that is the closest to receive the coming Messiah. However, such physical distance doesn't make it so you see Jesus Christ more closely. Only when you don't seek your own benefit, but achieve a clean heart that has no spot or blemish; pursue a good heart that sacrifices yourselves for others; and pursue peace with all men and achieve sanctification will you be qualified to see Jesus Christ in close proximity.

The Footsteps of Life

"And will come forth; those who did the good deeds to a resurrection of life,
 those who committed the evil deeds to a resurrection of judgment."
(John 5:29)

These days, we can see what wouldn't have
been seen otherwise through high-tech
video cameras or surveillance cameras. As
though with such technology, angels have
been recording all our deeds we do on the
earth. With this, the lives we led will be
revealed. With it as the evidence, God will
judge between good and evil. I hope you
will enjoy eternal life and joy by becoming
men and women of faith, love, and goodness
before God who searches all people with His
blazing eyes.

Unique Instinct

"For since the creation of the world His invisible attributes,
 His eternal power and divine nature, have been clearly seen,
 being understood through what has been made,
 so that they are without excuse."
(Romans 1:20)

Most animals have a unique instinct in common. It's known as the 'homing instinct'. The homing instinct refers to the ability of an animal, after being moved, stolen, or lost outside their established territory, to return to their home base. Likewise, God gives us men a spiritual homing instinct with which we long for our home, Heaven. So men of goodness feel the divinity and power of God and have hope for eternal life and accept Jesus Christ seeing heavens and earth and all things in them. In the end, they will go to the eternal Heaven.

Sincere Heart

"Let us draw near with a sincere heart in full assurance of faith,
having our hearts sprinkled clean from an evil conscience
and our bodies washed with pure water."
(Hebrews 10:22)

Men's true value and dignity don't come from
external factors like wealth, fame, knowledge,
appearance, and the like. Even though some
have many things, if they have crafty hearts,
selfish motives, greed, and arrogance, they
are not valuable, and should be ashamed.
Only those who achieve clean, precious, and
true hearts can recover the dignity of men
who were formed in the image of God. A
true heart refers to the heart with no lying
at all. It doesn't change due to circumstances
or condition. It is filled with sincere faith
towards God and is a holy and noble heart
absent of change for personal advantage.

All Kinds of Blessings

"The young lions do lack and suffer hunger;
  but they who seek the LORD shall not be in want of any good thing."
(Psalm 34:10)

People have the different standards of blessing. Some might treasure money while others might treasure health or peace in the family. But even if you have gained one of these standards, it's not enough to say you are a blessed man. For example, someone may have peace in family, but he is in poverty. Another may be rich but has a serious disease. They cannot say they are blessed. However, you can enjoy all kinds of blessing in God. You will not only receive salvation and go to Heaven but you will also receive all good things to the extent that you love God and live in the 66 books of the Bible. I hope you will become a person who enjoys all kinds of blessing in the God of love.

"Then God blessed the seventh day and sanctified it,
because in it He rested from all His work which God had created and made."

Genesis 2:3

Part 7

Hope for Heaven

Special Day of Rest

"For six days work may be done, but on the seventh day
you shall have a holy day, a sabbath of complete rest to the LORD;
whoever does any work on it shall be put to death."
(Exodus 35:2)

Once in America, many people moved westward to dig for gold. Among them, unbelievers didn't take a rest on the way because they wanted to get gold in their hands quickly. So horses became weary and finally collapsed. People got sick. On the other hand, those who believed in God stopped their marching in order to keep the Lord's Day. They took a rest both in spirit and in body. Their horses remained strong and people were healthy. They reached the destination faster than unbelievers and succeeded as pioneers of the land. When we work hard for six days and give service to God on the seventh day, we can have rest both in spirit and body and even receive blessing of all things becoming prosperous.

Because We Have Hope

"Jesus said to her, 'I am the resurrection and the life;
  he who believes in Me will live even if he dies, and everyone who lives
  and believes in Me will never die. Do you believe this?'"
(John 11:25-26)

Our life doesn't end on this earth. There is definitely an afterlife in either Heaven or Hell. When those who have accepted the Lord and have faith die, they will be resurrected on the last day and enjoy eternal life in Heaven. That's why the Bible says those believers who breathed the last breath are not 'dead' but 'asleep.' Just as people who sleep wake up in the morning, those believers will be resurrected on the final day. Other believers who are alive will meet Jesus Christ at His Second Coming without seeing death. Their bodies will change into spiritual bodies in a moment and be caught up into the air. Thanks overflow in such a Christian life filled with such hope.

Peace in the Heart

"The LORD lift up His countenance on you,
and give you peace."
(Numbers 6:26)

After Jesus was crucified, His disciples were
in anxiety and worried in deep sorrow for the
loss and in fear of Jewish persecutions. But
Jesus, who had put on the resurrected body,
appeared before them saying, "Peace be with
you." Right then, doubts and fear left them
and they came to have faith in and hope for
the resurrection. Afterwards, they preached
the gospel without fear even of death. When
they had no faith, they were fearful. But,
after they had faith and hope they came to
have true peace. Even today, there are two
kinds of people when it comes to faith. It is
the Christians who have true faith and hope
for Heaven who enjoy peace in their hearts
transcending circumstances and conditions.

When You Start to Attend Church

"And the Scripture was fulfilled which says,
'And Abraham believed God, and it was reckoned to him
as righteousness,' and he was called the friend of God.'"
(James 2:23)

When I was a beginner in faith, after a long time my brother visited my home. While we were having a conversation, my wife set the table for our meal. I said to him, "Now I am a Christian, so I can't serve you alcohol." This hurt his feelings. When you start a Christian life, relations with your close friends might go sour and you might feel lonely because of it. But the more you lean your heart toward God the more joy that the world cannot give will overflow in you. Such joy will be a driving force to lead your family, relatives, friends, and neighbors to the arms of God.

Love is Patient

"Love is patient, love is kind and is not jealous;
  love does not brag and is not arrogant."
(1 Corinthians 13:4)

One of the characteristics of love is patience.
If you lack patience many troubles can occur.
For example, if a superior isn't patient, he
might immediately take a job away from
his subordinate when good performance
hasn't been demonstrated. The subordinate
doesn't have a chance to make up for his
mistake and shortcoming, but just falls into
despair, blaming his inadequacy. However,
God puts an emphasis on patience. It is a
basic condition that we must have in order
to achieve love. Keeping patient with love
is never difficult to you. It is different from
patience without love because with love we
can believe that they will change.

Hidden Jewels

"Blessed are the poor in spirit,
  for theirs is the kingdom of heaven."
(Matthew 5:3)

Kites and hawks have eyes so sharp that they can see a small animal from great heights in the sky. While they are flying in the sky, they descend quickly as soon as they see their prey. They snap into it with their claws and ascend into the sky again. However, birds with such good eyes cannot see gemstones among the rocks. It's just like people not being able to realize the value of God's words like the precious gemstones when they are blinded by the worldly things like fame, authority, and wealth.

Praise with Fragrance

"O sing to the LORD a new song, for He has done wonderful things,
His right hand and His holy arm have gained the victory for Him."
(Psalm 98:1)

Many people prefer a flower in the field to fabulous-looking artificial flowers. This is because the flower in the field has life and fragrance. In this same way, God loves praise filled with fragrance. It is praise that is sung not just with a beautiful voice, but sung from the bottom of our hearts with joy, thanks, and love for Him, by living in the Word of God. Such praises give comfort and joy to those who are sad and heal broken-hearts and give them strength to overcome sufferings. They can also receive the help of God and answers from Him. It serves as the gate of blessings.

A Happy Christian Life

"Come to Me, all who are weary and heavy-laden,
  and I will give you rest."
(Matthew 11:28)

While hiking in the mountains, we feel like our backpack becomes heavier over time. Then, we can begin to throw away the useless things with no regret. It's the same with our getting rid of sin and evil from our hearts. If you discover hatred, jealousy, arrogance, and hot-temperament, you have to cast them away quickly. The more you discover, the more you should be pleased. It is because you can have peace and receive God-prepared blessings to the extent that you get rid of what you have discovered.

The Strength to Change

"See how great a love the Father has bestowed on us,
that we would be called children of God; and such we are.
For this reason the world does not know us, because it did not know Him."
(1 John 3:1)

Many children grow up without receiving love from parents or other people. They lack self-confidence and even have hostility towards the world. They are usually pessimistic about themselves. But such children can change amazingly when they experience God's love. God loves them not only when they do well but also when they don't do well. He even encourages them more with His mercy. He holds them until the end even when everybody turns away from them. With such love, they come to have self-confidence thinking "I am a being who is loved" and they become renewed.

One who Knows His Position

"Do not speak against one another, brethren.
 He who speaks against a brother or judges his brother,
 speaks against the law and judges the law; but if you judge the law,
 you are not a doer of the law but a judge of it."
(James 4:11)

The 'position' of someone or something is the place where they are in relation to other things. If you are arrogant, you might say things not considering where you are in relation to others around you or the situation. They can be words of judgment, condemnation, slandering, grudging, complaining, and blaming. As humans who are 'creatures' we have no right to speak such things. The right to pass judgment and condemnation only belongs to God the Creator. Therefore, if we speak such words we fail to know our own position in relation to God. By God's grace, we are saved and can enter Heaven. But, if you complain or begrudge concerning the reality of your life, you forget about the great grace of salvation. Those who remember they've been taken from Hell and received the grace of salvation, namely, those who know their position with God, give thanks always under any circumstances.

Outward Appearances and the Heart

"Man looks at the outward appearance,
  but the LORD looks at the heart."
(1 Samuel 16:7)

There were people who kept the law on the outside but had corrupted hearts. Their hearts were filled with sins, so Jesus reproved them. They were Pharisees and scribes at the time of Jesus. Since they kept the traditions of elders, they regarded people who ate with unwashed hands impure before God. One day, they saw Jesus' disciples eating with unwashed hands. They were about to reprove them. Then, Jesus said, *"It is not what enters into the mouth that defiles the man, but what proceeds out of the mouth, this defiles the man"* (Matthew 15:11). What proceeds out of the mouth comes from hearts, which are evil thoughts, murder, adultery, harlotry, and stealing. God looks at the heart. He regards those who cast away evil from their hearts to have 'pure' hearts.

The Talent of Talents

"O love the LORD, all you His godly ones!
  The LORD preserves the faithful and fully recompenses the proud doer."
(Psalm 31:23)

A man was recorded in the Guinness Book as having climbed with their hands the Empire State Building in New York City, in the United States. Surprisingly, he had acrophobia. He said he could succeed to finish the climbing because he kept his courage he had mustered up at first with patience until the end. What about Joseph? He was sold into Egypt as a slave but he relied on God under any and all circumstances and unchangingly worked hard. He finally became a ruler of the country, only second to the king. There are many people who were born with outstanding talents in the world. But the more important talents are patience and courage that never give up, and attitudes to do their best. We need to have a humble heart of asking God for His help all the time.

Harmony

"So that there may be no division in the body,
  but that the members may have the same care for one another."
(1 Corinthians 12:25)

When we go to some famous restaurants gourmets love, we can find they have a special recipe even if the kinds of food are just the same as those of other restaurants. The secret is in the amount of ingredients and spices. Namely, they don't put a lot just because they are good. The taste depends on proper amount of ingredients and spices. It's the same with the relationship with other people. When those with different wisdom and knowledge are harmonized, they can create great things. In other words, they can improve and develop themselves when they don't insist on themselves and respect one another's opinions.

Self-reflection

"For this reason it says, 'Awake, sleeper, and arise from the dead, and Christ will shine on you.'"
(Ephesians 5:14)

A university in USA conducted an experiment. The researchers put a frog in cold water and brought the water's temperature slowly up to boiling. The frog enjoyed the water that was getting warmer, but it ended up dying in the boiling water. There are people who pass judgment and condemnation on others and hate them without them even knowing it. Just as the frog missed the chance to get out of the hot water, we cannot help but stay far from the love of God when we pile up evil in our hearts by words, thoughts and deeds, even if they are too small to notice. So we need to reflect upon ourselves in the light of the Bible.

The Truth in the Bible

"Seek from the book of the LORD, and read:
Not one of these will be missing; none will lack its mate.
For His mouth has commanded, and His Spirit has gathered them."
(Isaiah 34:16)

The Bible tells us in one place that a robber on one side insulted Jesus when He was crucified. Another place in the Bible says two robbers on both sides insulted Him. Why was this difference recorded in the Bible? When a disciple who was in the crowd looked at the scene, it looked like both robbers were insulting Him when in fact, one of the robbers didn't insult Jesus but rebuked another robber on the other side for his insulting remarks toward Jesus. From one viewpoint it looked like both of them insulted Him because one of them on his cross just turned his face to the robber on the other side of Jesus. At that time, there was no audio-visual recording equipment. So God let the scene be described in different ways so that people would be able to understand the situation where a large number of people gathered under the cross. One disciple couldn't hear the conversation because he was too far from the cross. The other could hear. As you know, the Word of God written in the Bible has no error at all.

Spirit, Soul, and Body

"He has made everything appropriate in its time.
He has also set eternity in their heart, yet so that man will not find out
the work which God has done from the beginning even to the end."
(Ecclesiastes 3:11)

Some say that human cloning is possible because they have succeeded in animal cloning. But human beings cannot create the male's sperm and female's eggs. Even if science develops even more, the spirit of a man cannot be cloned. Even if cells can be cloned and the image of a man can be created, a body without a spirit and a soul is but a dead person. Since men have spirit and soul, they can think and speak, and find the Deity with longing hearts, which makes us different from animals. Therefore, the body of man is like a container for the spirit and soul. The real master of men is spirit in the body.

A Dream

"But as it is, they desire a better country that is, a heavenly one.
Therefore God is not ashamed to be called their God;
for He has prepared a city for them."
(Hebrews 11:16)

People liken vanity in life to an 'empty dream'. No matter how fantastic the dream is, you will wake up from the dream at a point. If you thought that it was real, how void and empty you would feel when you woke up! Likewise, there are some people who feel like their life is only a one-night's-dream. When they end their life on the earth, no matter how great the wealth and fame they enjoyed it was only a dream. Our life on the earth is short, but a true life of all people is eternal, and it can be in Heaven. Therefore, those who are well-prepared for the true life in Heaven will enjoy eternal joy of the real life in Heaven when they are awakened from 'the life on the earth.'

More Important
than the Outcome

"He must turn away from evil and do good;
  He must seek peace and pursue it."
(1 Peter 3:11)

When they were celebrating a national holiday, the children gathered together at one place. The eldest son, who was rich, said to his other siblings, "Why don't you be the ones who buy the presents for our parents next time?" He was actually rebuking them. The parents became concerned for their other children. Parents still want their children to get along well, even if they don't bring anything as presents for them. God does the same. Let's say a person pushes a matter forward insisting on his opinion. He might say, "I have no other choice but do this in order to achieve great things". But it is far from God's heart which is love itself. God delights in the heart of love and peace shown in any process rather than merely the outcome.

Two Angels in White

"In Him we have redemption through His blood,
 the forgiveness of our trespasses, according to the riches of His grace."
(Ephesians 1:7)

In many cases, people see the spiritual world when their spiritual eyes are opened just before they take their last breath. At that time, they see two angels welcoming those who receive salvation. The two angels lead them to the heavenly kingdom. The two angels wait for their spirits and show the way to the heavenly kingdom after the last breath. Seeing the two angels in the light, the saved souls close their eyes with a smile and in peace. On the contrary, those who don't receive salvation, but go to Hell, are suddenly struck by fear, seeing the spiritual world they face just before their death. Then, what facial expressions and reactions should we have when we end this life on the earth? We have to accept Jesus Christ and become blessed people who can reach the heavenly kingdom guided by the two angels in white.

The Letter of Christ

"You are our letter, written in our hearts, known and read by all men;
  being manifested that you are a letter of Christ."
(2 Corinthians 3:2-3)

E-mail is commonly used these days for much
of our written communication today, but do
you remember the handwritten letters when
there were no computers? You are moved by
such letters from sons in the army or friends
in overseas countries if you have waited for
it to arrive for a long time. The Bible calls
believers "The Letters of Christ" because
many people listen to the Word of God from
believers and feel the love of God through
their good deeds. Jesus redeemed us from
our sins with the love of the cross and He
gave us the opportunity for eternal life. But
only those who can receive the 'letter of Jesus
Christ' with joy can also receive the blessing
of eternal life.

The Best Fruit

"His winnowing fork is in His hand, and He will thoroughly clear
His threshing floor; and He will gather His wheat into the barn,
but He will burn up the chaff with unquenchable fire."
(Matthew 3:12)

When farmers harvest fruit in the fall, its quality
varies. Some of the fresh fruit is worthy to receive
a good price in the market, but some isn't. There is
also some that is neither good enough to sell in the
market nor bad enough to throw away. So they just
put it in a warehouse. In the past, the best fruit was
reserved for kings. Likewise, God's saved children
are all different from person to person. Of course,
all of them enter the heavenly kingdom, but the
extent that God is pleased is different according to
how good a piece of fruit they are. That's why the
heavenly dwelling places and heavenly rewards are
different. Good fruit refers to those who become
sanctified by abiding in the Word of God. Think
about how good your fruit is in the sight of God
who is the Master of your spirit and soul.

Let's Overcome the Limit

"I, the LORD, am your God, who brought you up
  from the land of Egypt; open your mouth wide and I will fill it."
(Psalm 81:10)

Peter let his nets out in the water and worked hard all night but he caught nothing. Jesus said to him, *"Put out into the deep water and let down your nets for a catch"* (Luke 5:4). Peter had been a fisherman for a long time, which means he had a lot of experience, but he obeyed Jesus' word and let down his nets in deep water. Then, he caught a great quantity of fish. Just as Martin Luther said, "Let God be God," we must not confine the limitless power of God in the frameworks of human beings. Anyone who relies on God the Almighty can experience miracles beyond human knowledge and limitations.

God is Love

"Know therefore that the LORD your God, He is God, the faithful God,
who keeps His covenant and His lovingkindness to a thousandth generation
with those who love Him and keep His commandments."
(Deuteronomy 7:9)

We feel happy when we see the beautiful
creatures of the heavens and the earth—
everything in them. We find happiness in the
goodness found in the hearts of others. How
happy you will be if you achieve the heart of
God who is the origin of all beauty, goodness,
and love! God-given love is peace that sets us
free from pain, and it is also brightness and
hope that drive the dark away as well. It is joy
that casts out sorrow and it is comfort that
wipes tears away. It is also the source of vitality
that lightens our body and hearts when we
are weary and experience times of difficulty. I
hope you will enjoy each day filled with true
peace and joy in the love of God.

The Lamp of Life

"Your word is a lamp to my feet and a light to my path."
(Psalm 119:105)

Just like lamps that shed light on the streets
in the dark of night, the Word of God
sheds light that tells us what to do in this
complicated world and guides us to the right
way. In the Word of God are solutions to all
problems and ways and understandings. God
foreknows everything, and He had the first
chapter and the last chapter of human life to
be recorded in the Bible. How good it will
be if we commit our lives to God who knows
everything and can do everything! The way
to spend the time given to us on the earth in
a precious way is to gain understanding from
the Word of God, thinking about it as the
lamp of life.

The Author
Dr. Jaerock Lee

Dr. Jaerock Lee was born in Muan, Jeonnam Province, Republic of Korea, in 1943. In his twenties, Dr. Lee suffered from a variety of incurable diseases for seven years and awaited death with no hope for recovery. One day in the spring of 1974, however, he was led to a church by his sister and when he knelt down to pray, the living God immediately healed him of all his diseases.

From the moment Dr. Lee met the living God through that wonderful experience, he has loved God with all his heart and sincerity, and in 1978 he was called to be a servant of God. He prayed fervently with countless fasting prayers so that he could clearly understand the will of God, wholly accomplish it and obey the Word of God. In 1982, he founded Manmin Central Church in Seoul, Korea, and countless works of God, including miraculous healings, signs and wonders, have been taking place at his church.

In 1986, Dr. Lee was ordained as a pastor at the Annual Assembly of Jesus' Sungkyul Church of Korea, and four years later in 1990, his sermons began to be broadcast in Australia, Russia, the Philippines, and many more through the Far East Broadcasting Company, the Asia Broadcast Station, and the Washington Christian Radio System.

Three years later in 1993, Manmin Central Church was selected as one of the "World's Top 50 Churches" by the Christian World magazine (US) and he received an Honorary Doctorate of Divinity from Christian Faith College, Florida, USA, and in 1996 a Ph. D. in Ministry from Kingsway Theological Seminary, Iowa, USA.

Since 1993, Dr. Lee has been spearheading world evangelization through many overseas crusades in Tanzania, Argentina, L.A., Baltimore City, Hawaii, and New York City of the USA, Uganda, Japan, Pakistan, Kenya, the Philippines, Honduras, India, Russia, Germany, Peru, Democratic Republic of the Congo, Israel and Estonia.

In 2002 he was called a "worldwide revivalist" by major Christian newspapers in Korea for his powerful ministries in various overseas crusades. Especially, his

'New York Crusade 2006' held in Madison Square Garden, the most world-famous arena, was broadcast to 220 nations, and in his 'Israel United Crusade 2009' held in International Convention Center in Jerusalem he boldly proclaimed Jesus Christ is the Messiah and Savior. His sermon is brodacst to 176 nations via satellites including GCN TV and he was listed as one of the Top 10 Most Influential Christian Leaders of 2009 and 2010 by the Russian popular Christian magazine *In Victory* and new agency *Christian Telegraph* for his powerful TV broadcasting ministry and overseas church-pastoring ministry.

As of July of 2012, Manmin Central Church has a congregation of more than 120,000 members. There are 10,000 branch churches throughout the globe including 56 domestic branch churches, and so far more than 129 missionaries have been commissioned to 23 countries, including the United States, Russia, Germany, Canada, Japan, China, France, India, Kenya, and many more.

As of the date of this publishing, Dr. Lee has written 64 books, including bestsellers *Tasting Eternal Life before Death*, *My Life My Faith I & II*, *The Message of the Cross*, *The Measure of Faith*, *Heaven I & II*, *Hell*, *Awaken Israel*, and *The Power of God*. His works have been translated into more than 74 languages.

His Christian columns appear on *The Hankook Ilbo*, *The JoongAng Daily*, *The Chosun Ilbo*, *The Dong-A Ilbo*, *The Munhwa Ilbo*, *The Seoul Shinmun*, *The Kyunghyang Shinmun*, *The Hankyoreh Shinmun*, *The Korea Economic Daily*, *The Korea Herald*, *The Shisa News*, and *The Christian Press*.

Dr. Lee is currently leader of many missionary organizations and associations: including Chairman, The United Holiness Church of Jesus Christ; President, Manmin World Mission; Permanent President, The World Christianity Revival Mission Association; Founder & Board Chairman, Global Christian Network (GCN); Founder & Board Chairman, World Christian Doctors Network (WCDN); and Founder & Board Chairman, Manmin International Seminary (MIS).

Heaven I & II

A detailed sketch of the gorgeous living environment the heavenly citizens enjoy and beautiful description of different levels of heavenly kingdoms.

The Message of the Cross

A powerful awakening message for all the people who are spiritually asleep! In this book you will find the reason Jesus is the only Savior and the true love of God.

Hell

An earnest message to all mankind from God, who wishes not even one soul to fall into the depths of hell! You will discover the never-before-revealed account of the cruel reality of the Lower Grave and Hell.

My Life My Faith I & II

Dr. Jaerock Lee's autobiography provides the most fragrant spiritual aroma for the readers, through his life extracted from the love of God blossomed in midst of the dark waves, cold yoke and the deepest despair.

The Measure of Faith

What kind of a dwelling place, crown and reward are prepared for you in heaven? This book provides with wisdom and guidance for you to measure your faith and cultivate the best and most mature faith.